Letters of Love

Letters of Love

Sermons and Reflections

by

Mark and Sandy Jerstad

Zion Publishing
Des Moines, Iowa

ISBN: 978-0-9627147-7-1

Published by
Zion Publishing
1500 Crown Colony Court #540
Des Moines, Iowa 50315

Distributed by
The Jerstad Family Foundation
1-605-261-1044

Printed in the United States of America

To Mark,

Whose love filled my life with meaning and joy, and whose friendship bound us together in continual conversation;

Whose powerful words continue to inspire me and others to dream big and spend our lives for the sake of our brothers and sisters;

Who left me with rich memories and the unparalleled joy of children and grandchildren;

Whose legacy of The Jerstad Family Foundation continues to unite our family through giving to others in need.

Acknowledgements

- To my children—Rachel, Mike and Sarah, and daughter-in-law Kelly—whose love, help, and support have meant the world to me;
- To my grandchildren: Sarah K., Joe, Elizabeth, Luke, Christian and Catherine, who bring love, laughter, and inspiration into my life;
- To my mother-in-law Laura whose love and friendship anchor me and whose validation of this book encouraged me;
- To my editor/publisher Mary Nilsen without whose expertise and guidance this book would never have become a reality;
- To Senator Tom Daschle for writing the Foreword and to Dr. James Limburg and Rev. Dr. Greg Wilcox for years of friendship and support of this project;
- To Marianne Larsen for photographs used this book;
- To my proof readers for their careful work: Shirley Halleen, Cathy Piersol, Linda Pashby, Jean Nicholson, Maryanne Petersen, and Julie Tibbets;
- To Juli Peterson and Rob Nelson for providing me with invaluable assistance with computer problems—

To all of these and many more, I give my heartfelt thanks.

Sandy Jerstad

Table of Contents

Prologue

We all have goals for the future, for the someday that may never happen. One of those goals for my husband, Mark, was to put together a book of some of the sermons that he preached at Augustana College between 1977 and 1984, editing them to make them timeless. He died before accomplishing this goal, so I decided several years ago to take on the project. Before I began, I was elected to the South Dakota State Senate, which kept me busy. But winter of 2011 was the perfect time to begin reading and writing.

Editing Mark's sermons and creating this book has given me great joy. As I read his old sermons and reflected on them, I saw his big smile, felt his arms around me, and heard his voice. Eventually, I gave myself permission to talk back to his sermons through my reflections—to talk about him, about our life together, and the sermon itself. This sweet journey into the past has been a satisfying, fulfilling task, one I hope will bring wisdom and joy, insight and a deeper commitment to life and to faith for all who read it. Mark believed words have power. Whether you knew Mark or not, whether you ever heard him preach or not, I hope his power, his essence, his love of life and of God will move you as you read his sermons and my reflections.

Mark and I met briefly toward the end of my freshman year at St. Olaf College in Northfield, Minnesota, and something about him, something hard to describe but compelling, made me decide that when I returned to college for my sophomore year, he was the one man I wanted to date. My dream came true the following fall. One crisp afternoon, with leaves crunching around our feet, we took a walk together. As we headed toward his car parked off campus, he told me he was looking for a wife.

When I heard those words I knew two things: He was just chatting, and I wanted it to be me. Since flirting was never one of my strong suits, I had trouble getting Mark to notice me, really notice me, and ask me out for a date. When my roommates finally persuaded me to ask Mark out for Girls Date Night, and I finally set out to do so, I had to pursue him all the way across campus in order to find him not surrounded by girls. He was gracious and perceptive in the face of my stumbling invitation to go to the play, *Summer and Smoke*, and he immediately asked me out to a concert to be held prior to the evening of the play. We both felt the chemistry that night at the concert, casually entwining our little fingers together as we walked out.

Mark and I were married in my hometown of Virginia, Minnesota, on August 21, 1965. I still had to finish my senior year at St. Olaf and he was going to Luther Seminary, so I commuted to Northfield from our tiny basement apartment near the seminary for six weeks, and then I did my practice teaching in Roseville at a middle school nearby. I finished my college degree after interim (January), in three and a half years, and went to work teaching at Osseo Jr. High.

Mark finished his second year at Luther, and we headed off for his internship in Seattle, where I taught 9th grade English at a challenging inner-city school. Back in St. Paul the following year, I returned to Roseville, this time as a certified teacher, and Mark completed the Seminary and decided to go on with his studies at Union Theological Seminary in Richmond, Virginia. I loved that year—the weather was perfect, the people were welcoming, and, most important, our first child, Rachel, was born.

Although his professors wanted him to stay on to work toward a PhD in biblical studies, at the end of the first year Mark decided he needed to get his feet wet in parish ministry. After six months of waiting and working part-time jobs while staying with my mother in Virginia, Minnesota, we took a call to International Falls, Minnesota. Yes, it is the coldest place in the 48 States. Winter began in October and lasted until May. I used to call my friend Pat to go cross-country skiing through the woods as late as April.

Mike and Sarah were born there, and three children under the age of five kept me busy. I also found some wonderful friends, who were treasures. Audrey and Joe Dahl took us in like family. Ruby and Bill Skwarok accompanied me on pre-dawn walks even when the temperature was a nostril-flaring 30° below. Pat and I shared kid care, cooking, and a lifetime of heart-felt stories, which helped both of us endure the endless winters. And because Mark worked all the time, pouring love and attention into the congregation, everyone grew to love him.

But after seven years as a small town pastor, Mark was ready for something new, so, in 1977, he accepted a call to become campus pastor at Augustana College in Sioux Falls, South Dakota. We moved our small family to Sioux Falls after Christmas and began a new life.

Because Mark had taken a pay cut to work at Augustana, I had to go to work and was offered a part-time job teaching inmates in the school at the state penitentiary in town. Surprisingly, I loved it.

Then one day a senior coed, Pam Johnson, visited Mark in his office, and he found out she played three sports a year and was about to start her last season in softball. However, the team did not have a coach. Ever the optimist, Mark reported to her that his wife could do that, and she reported it to the athletic director, who immediately offered me a contract for $500 to coach softball.

With that event, my life changed. I started taking classes at Augustana to complete a major in health, physical education, and recreation. With that completed, I commuted to South Dakota State University several times a week to complete a master's degree in health, physical education and recreation, the prerequisite for me for accepting a full-time coaching position at Augie.

Meanwhile, Mark was preaching three times a week, twice at chapel and once on Sunday. I loved his sermons. He was a charismatic speaker, and his sermons had staying power. Before long, the facility of the old gym, which doubled as the worship service area, was packed with students. Mark spearheaded a fund-raising drive to build a real chapel on campus, and when it was complete, chapel was offered four days a week. More chances to preach.

Mark had a special way with words and was able to connect on a personal level with his audience. Sometimes it felt as if he was talking directly to you. Often he was animated, and stories permeated his sermons. There were no wireless microphones in those days, so he held a microphone with a very long cord to accommodate his wandering around the front of the chapel as he spoke.

One Sunday as he spoke and walked back and forth, the long cord began to wind around his legs. Everyone wanted to tell him, but no one did. All of a sudden he stopped and looked down at the cord wound around his body. "This is what happens to us in life—we get all wound up in ourselves and our busy lives and forget God and his love for us." It was a sermon illustration, artfully executed. No one suspected. No one ever forgot it.

Mark put himself in his sermons, and he never hesitated to tell stories about his family, either. He did it in a way that grounded the sermons in reality and illustrated the Gospel. He used down-to-earth illustrations and humor, and because he told stories to emphasize his points, he usually accomplished his three goals in every sermon or talk: make them laugh, make them cry, and make them remember one thing.

Because he was a voracious reader, he often quoted authors, and since he was a minister, with a high-pressured schedule, sometimes he gave the same sermon multiple times, of course in different locations. Usually I enjoyed that, like a child who wants to hear the same story over and over again, but sometimes I felt the stories were too sad or too personal. One story he related about the delivery of our son was a beautiful, sacred time, but one I would have preferred to keep private and personal.

In 1981, Mark was recruited by St. Olaf College to become the next campus pastor, with an additional offer to become a full professor. He went through a wrenching decision-making process lasting for several months. He had dreamed about that job at his alma mater and thought that was where he had always wanted to go.

And yet, there was something else tugging at him—a deep desire to one day work for Good Samaritan, the long-term care organization his grandfather had started with pennies in 1922 in Arthur, North Dakota. He believed if he went to St. Olaf he would never leave. So he made the decision to stay at Augustana with no assurance that his dream of working at Good Samaritan would come to fruition.

But it did. In 1985, Good Samaritan hired him to head up human resources. Two years later he took on the COO position, and in 1989 was hired by the Board of Directors to be the next president and CEO. He was ecstatic! He had his dream job.

Just seven years later, on March 29, 1997, he died of colon cancer. But during those years he made big things happen at Good Samaritan. He brought the company into the computer age, instituted a master's program for administrators that they could complete while on the job, and reformed the investment program for the industry and the workers. In addition, he planned a whole campus of new buildings, including a retreat center with sleeping and eating facilities, a huge great room for daily devotions, meeting rooms of all kinds, and a chapel.

Under his leadership, the society also purchased a new facility—the building abandoned by the Bank of New York. In addition, they purchased 40 acres in the same area, which is now home to a beautiful development of twin homes with a walking path and a creek running through it, a lodge with rental units, and an assisted living facility. Mark had planned all these things before his untimely death, and had lined up a very talented architect from Minneapolis who had created designs for the initial building.

During this time he traveled a great deal, visiting the Good Samaritan facilities, all 240 scattered around the US, and attending board meetings for the American Health Care Association in Washington, DC. He was a sought-after speaker as well, for both church and business organizations.

Editing his sermons has been an all-consuming project that I have loved. I have learned a great deal from my editor, Mary Nilsen, and have heard Mark's sermons again in a new way, a way that drew me close both to him and to God. But most important, my hope and prayer is that this book will touch and inspire those who open its cover and absorb its words. I also hope it will help my grandchildren come to know the grandfather they never met.

I have included in this collection a speech by Mark's good friend, Senator Tom Daschle, and, at the end of the book, an Argus Leader article by Steve Young, both of which Senator Daschle entered into the Congressional Record on February 4th, 1997. Through them you will learn more about Mark and how he faced his own death.

Sandy Jerstad

Foreword

Death is nothing at all—
I have only slipped away into the next room.
Whatever we were to each other, that we are still.
Call me by my old familiar name, speak to me in the easy
  way which we always used.
Laugh as we always laughed at the little jokes we enjoyed
  together.
Play, smile, think of me, pray for me.
Let my name be the household word it always was.
Let it be spoken without effort.
Life means all that it ever meant.
It is the same as it always was:
There is an absolute unbroken continuity.
Why would I be out of your mind because I am out of
  your sight?
I am but waiting for you, for an interval, somewhere very
  near, just around the corner.
All is well. Nothing is passed, nothing is lost.
One brief moment, and all will be as it was before—
Only better, infinitely happier, and forever—
We will all be one together with Christ.

"Togetherness"—An Irish text found in a Carmelite
Monastery in Tallow County, Wicklow, Ireland

I have always found strength in these words especially at times when I struggle with the loss of someone I love. My strength comes in realizing their truth. I find extraordinary solace and comfort in accepting these truths partly in faith but also in fact. As the wisdom of Wicklow reminds us, those whom we love before death are loved equally afterwards.

And it is our faith that allows us to share the gift of knowing that after "one brief moment" all will be as it was before.

As I read the beautiful words of Mark and Sandy Jerstad, I am reminded that they continue to give "togetherness" in this context fresh meaning.

They always have.

I vividly remember things, as they were before, with Mark and Sandy. I have known them for nearly three decades. Perhaps not surprisingly, it was politics that brought us together. They were supporters of mine and quickly became very special friends.

I well remember, after our first meeting, I immediately thought of them as the perfect couple. I soon learned that many others shared my perception. Young, energetic, widely respected, they were viewed by nearly everyone as future superstars in the community.

Mark was an extremely popular pastor and professor of religion at Augustana College in Sioux Falls, South Dakota. His intellectual sermons and lectures were widely recognized as both thought provoking and resonant with growing audiences in church and in college.

In spite of his love for the church and the classroom, Mark later decided to dedicate his professional life to improving health care. In 1989, he joined the Good Samaritan Society with over two hundred long-term health care facilities in more than twenty states. Later he became their extraordinarily successful President and CEO until his death in 1997.

Sandy was one of the most remarkable coaches in South Dakota history. She coached volleyball, tennis and softball, while teaching several classes at Augustana. Incredibly, she compiled a record of over 1000 wins. She was only the second coach in all NCAA divisions to do so.

They were married for thirty-one years and had three beautiful children, Rachel, Mike and Sarah, each of whom has become a very successful young adult.

In recent years, Sandy has served in the South Dakota State Legislature and on the boards of the Good Samaritan Society, the Banquet and the Center for Western Studies. She now has six grandchildren, Sarah, Joe, Elizabeth, Luke, Christian and Catherine.

Francis of Assisi was once asked what a person must do to lead a good life.

He answered, "Preach the Gospel everyday. If necessary, use words."

My admiration and affection for Mark and Sandy have grown enormously over time as I learned from their example. Each of them has lived St. Francis' admonition. They preached the Gospel as they dedicated their lives not only to each other and their family but also to a better community, a better country and a better world.

Just as Francis of Assisi found it necessary to use words, so have they. It began with Mark's inspirational sermons to his fortunate and grateful audiences. At the recommendation of many who heard him, he had decided to publish his sermons in order to give more people an opportunity to read them, too.

In the spirit of the togetherness that they lived for more than thirty years, Sandy made the decision to write her own reflections after each sermon. In a note to me she described these reflections as "somewhat of a memoir, covering a bit of family life, our relationship, my work in the Senate and at Augustana."

One of Mark's sermons was entitled "What Happens After Death?" Mark delivered it on November 7th, 1982. After quoting two compelling biblical passages from John and I Corinthians on the subject, he shared his own, wise counsel.

"There is a strain running through the whole biblical message that comes at us from our future and penetrates our now. This is what we call an eschatological promise, a promise that beyond this life there is something more, a gift that is given to us who are God's children and who believe in him. We are people of promise. We live in the hope and the promise given to us by God himself through Jesus Christ, that beyond this life we will be ushered into a new kingdom, another kingdom. That is my hope for each one of us."

Sandy responded to Mark's sermon with her own beautiful and poignant eloquence.

"Throughout typing this sermon, I could not help but think of Mark's dying and death, and what happened afterwards. During his illness the emotions of grief and hope made my heart and throat ache on a daily basis. Toward the end, I could hardly bear to watch him continue to suffer, but neither could I stand to think of life without him. When all the tubes and machines were finally wheeled away I crawled into bed with him and held him close, softly telling him he was going to the arms of God and that we would be OK."

On February 4th, 1997, I spoke on the floor of the United States Senate in tribute to Mark and his remarkable life. I noted that his ability to help others confront their fears and prepare for their next journey has always been based on his strong faith.

It was his faith that enabled Mark to be at peace with his own death knowing that, one day, he would be reunited with each of those he loved so dearly.

He told Steve Young, a reporter for the Sioux Falls Argus Leader, "One of the things that fires me up is knowing I'll get the chance to meet my dad again. He died a couple of years ago. I loved him dearly. What a glorious reunion."

Mark may have slipped into the next room. But as the old Irish text reminds us, and Sandy's words in this beautiful book confirm, all is well. Nothing is lost. Nothing is past.

Tom Daschle

Sermons and Reflections

Listen

Help carry one another's burdens, and in this way you will obey the law of Christ. Galatians 6:2

    5 During the time when Herod was king of Judea, there was a priest named Zechariah, who belonged to the priestly order of Abijah. His wife's name was Elizabeth; she also belonged to a priestly family. 6 They both lived good lives in God's sight and obeyed fully all the Lord's laws and commands. 7 They had no children because Elizabeth could not have any, and she and Zechariah were both very old. 8 One day Zechariah was doing his work as a priest in the Temple, taking his turn in the daily service. 9 According to the custom followed by the priests, he was chosen by lot to burn incense on the altar. So he went into the Temple of the Lord, 10 while the crowd of people outside prayed during the hour when the incense was burned. 11 An angel of the Lord appeared to him, standing at the right side of the altar where the incense was burned. 12 When Zechariah saw him, he was alarmed and felt afraid. 13 But the angel said to him, "Don't be afraid, Zechariah! God has heard your prayer, and your wife Elizabeth will bear you a son. You are to name him John. 14 How glad and happy you will be, and how happy many others will be when he is born! 15 John will be great in the Lord's sight. He must not drink any wine or strong drink. From his very birth he will be filled with the Holy Spirit, 16 and he will bring back many of the people of Israel to the Lord their God. 17 He will go ahead of the Lord, strong and mighty like the prophet Elijah. He will bring fathers and children together again; he will turn disobedient people back to the way of thinking of the righteous; he will get the Lord's people ready for him." 18 Zechariah said to the angel, "How shall I know if this is so? I am an old man, and my wife is old also." 19 "I am Gabriel," the angel answered. "I stand in the presence of God, who sent me to speak to you and tell you this good news. 20 But you have not believed my message, which will come true at the right time. Because you have not believed, you will be unable to speak; you will remain silent until the day my promise to you comes true." 21 In the meantime the people were waiting for Zechariah and wondering why he was spending such a long time in the Temple. 22 When he came out, he could not speak to them, and so they knew that he had seen a vision in the Temple. Unable to say a word, he made signs to them with his hands. Luke 1:5-22

If I were Elizabeth, I would have knelt down beside my bed that night and, after saying, "Now I lay me down to sleep," I would have whispered a special prayer. Not for the promise of a child in my old age. Not even for the special calling he was to be given. I would have whispered a special prayer of thanks for shutting my preacher husband up. Finally, after all these years, maybe he will listen to me.

Listen. Listen. Why is it so hard to listen? Heaven knows how crucial it is. Dietrich Bonhoeffer, in his beautiful little book, *Life Together*, tells us that the very first service that one owes to another consists in listening to them (p. 97).

Just as love for God begins with listening to his Word, so the beginning of love for one another is learning to listen. It is God's love for us that he not only gives us his word, but also lends us his ear. So it is his work that we do for our others when we learn to listen to them.

When we listen we are in effect saying, "I care, I'm interested, you are important." When we listen we are, in Paul's words, helping to carry one another's burdens.

We need to be reminded of this. From first year instructor to tenured professor, from freshman to graduate student, from neglected child to anguished and lonely housewife, from cook to keeper of the grounds to carpenter—people are looking for a listening ear, for someone who will help carry their burdens, share their sorrow and joy, struggle with them in times of doubt, pay attention, listen, listen, listen, listen.

What is our response? Far too often, it is talk, talk, talk. I have this picture in my mind of mouths, all kinds of mouths, jaws hinged and well-oiled, prattling at one another, and no ears, no listening.

What is the resolution of this ridiculous farce? Perhaps, for a start, many of us could use the treatment the angel of the Lord used on Zachariah, one good long human gestation period of silence. Lacking a visit from Michael or Gabriel or one of the other angels from the Heavenly Hosts, perhaps we could start by simply shutting up. And in that silence, listen. Listen for that still, small voice that Samuel heard, *"Speak, Lord, for your servant hears."*

Listen to that still small voice that gently reminds you that you do not need to prove your worth and value by the amount of verbal garbage you can pile up in your four score and ten. Listen to that still, small voice that comes to you from the mystery of eternity penetrating time—Jesus the Christ, who listens to you, lends you his ear, loves you, saves you, frees you, quiets you, and calls you to a ministry of listening, listening to your brother and sister.

You may never become a summa cum laude, Phi Beta Kappa, world-renowned novelist, full professor, PhD, but you can become a listener. And in so doing, carry one another's burdens. Listen. Listen. Listen!

Reflection

This was one of Mark's first sermons at Augustana after he was hired as campus pastor in January of 1977. Sunday service and twice-weekly chapel were held in the old gym, where I eventually had my office and where I had indoor practice for my softball team and my volleyball team. In this cathedral to sport, I took our kids to church, and we listened to Mark preach.

I can hardly explain or overstate what a gift editing these sermons has been for me. In these grounding devotional pieces, I hear my husband's voice and see his face, as I peck away at my computer in the room that used to be his study. Although this was one of his earliest sermons at Augustana, it was a gem. And he was a master at listening.

Besides being an exceptional preacher, Mark was a phenomenal counselor. I know this because many people have told me how much his counseling meant to them, how it changed their lives. In his office at Augustana, he would sit on the couch, curl his legs underneath him, (never mind that he was dressed to the nines in his suit) and direct his gaze at his visitor, making that person feel that he or she had his full attention, and listen. And as he listened, he helped that person move in a positive direction with his or her life.

One of the reasons I loved and married Mark was that he listened to me. It was not one-sided—I listened to him as well. In fact, our favorite pastime was to find a quiet little spot and share our thoughts about, well, about everything, from politics to theology to our daily work and, later on, of course, our children.

Long car rides flew by while we talked and listened to one another's thoughts, problems, and yearnings. We encouraged each other. I would never have had my 27-year career at Augustana, teaching and coaching, if Mark had not encouraged me to get my master's degree and apply for the full-time job.

When we were at St. Olaf together as students, it was common for us to meet at the cafeteria at 5 p.m. and, staring deeply into each other's eyes, talk our way through salad, chicken, desert, and multiple cups of not-so-good coffee, and still be talking and staring as tables were washed and all other diners headed for the library. When the work crew kicked us out, we promptly went to the coffee shop downstairs to continue our conversation.

During the two years Mark was at Luther Seminary, we came to know the territory surrounding our basement apartment in intimate detail, as we took long walks, talking about our day and our lives. Legs and mouths moved together, exercising our bodies and minds.

Later on, in International Falls, Minnesota, it was more difficult to take long walks with winter dominating much of the year. Beyond that, three children under five made leaving the house a challenge—with or without them. When the children were around, we would find an out of the way spot to close the door and ask that we not be disturbed. It was sacred time, and it happened in so many places: the car, the dock at the cabin, while we were out fishing, on a long walk or while biking, in our study at home or his study at work.

Most of the time these talks were peaceful and a joy. But once in a while problems arose between us needing to be ironed out and misunderstandings to address, misunderstandings that were not always resolved before bedtime. Sometimes passive-aggressive steely silences would last into the next day. But then one or the other of us would open our arms and hearts to the other, and the listening would begin all over.

Another obstacle to regular communication was Mark's work. He once charted out how many hours a week he was working to show to the church council. It was over 100 hours, not uncommon for a full-time solo pastor.

Part of the problem was his popularity with not only parishioners but also pretty much everyone in that small community who had a problem. When someone was dying in the hospital in the middle of the night, the nurse called Mark. She knew his presence would soothe and help the patient, his family, and the staff. Phone calls at 2:00 a.m. were not uncommon.

There were one-timers who called or came over, and there were the regulars. One night I had put the kids to bed and had a hot pizza in the oven, one of my homemade specials. We anticipated an hour or two of deep sharing over that pizza, getting our fingers greasy, laughing, and, of course, listening to the tales of each other's day.

Just as I pulled the pizza out of the oven, the doorbell rang. Mark welcomed in a young man, a problem drinker who was having family problems. Hours later, I am pretty sure I gave Mark a dirty look, as I passed by the living room on my way up to bed, the cold, uneaten pizza on the kitchen counter. There were too many of those times.

After seven years in International Falls, years filled with fascinating experiences and new friends, a call came for Mark to be campus pastor at Augustana College in Sioux Falls, South Dakota. Hard as it was to leave all those folks with whom we had shared so many intimate journeys, we felt excitement and anticipation, too.

I fell in love with the people at Augustana, especially the students. It is still that way. Mark did also and became the go-to guy on campus for students and faculty alike. An advantage was the scarcity of evening meetings and extra hours of counseling sessions. Our time together was so much more our own, and our family thrived in that togetherness. The campus became a cozy hangout for our children.

Since Mark had taken a cut in pay to become the campus pastor, he negotiated two months off in the summer, which our family spent on an island on Rainy Lake near International Falls—a sanctuary where there was no electricity or hot water but plenty of mice.

We had ample opportunity to listen—to the wind in the pine trees and the water lapping against our dock and boat, to the loons calling to each other at night and the thunder echoing up and down the lake, to the crackle of the fire in the big split rock fireplace we all had helped to build, and to each other.

Our children and now my grandchildren look forward to the trip to the cabin each summer—a time when life slows down and parents listen to their children, while dangling their feet in the water or sweating in the sauna or going fishing together. Family history is shared at meal times on the screen porch, and the important life questions of the children are given careful consideration.

I am grateful to Mark for choosing this cabin on Lost Bay and grateful to God for all the love shared through talking and listening from sunrise through sunset. In this place, which gently opens our hearts and souls and allows us to truly listen to one another and to our creator, we practice what we hope to bring to the rest of our lives—the power of listening.

Kelly and daughter Elizabeth

Called

1 In those days, when the boy Samuel was serving the Lord under the direction of Eli, there were very few messages from the Lord, and visions from him were quite rare. 2 One night Eli, who was now almost blind, was sleeping in his own room; 3 Samuel was sleeping in the sanctuary, where the sacred Covenant Box was. Before dawn, while the lamp was still burning, 4 the Lord called Samuel. He answered, "Yes, sir!" 5 and ran to Eli and said, "You called me, and here I am." But Eli answered, "I didn't call you; go back to bed." So Samuel went back to bed. 6 The Lord called Samuel again. The boy did not know that it was the Lord, because the Lord had never spoken to him before. So he got up, went to Eli, and said, "You called me, and here I am." But Eli answered, "My son, I didn't call you; go back to bed." 8 The Lord called Samuel a third time; he got up, went to Eli, and said, "You called me, and here I am." Then Eli realized that it was the Lord who was calling the boy, 9 so he said to him, "Go back to bed; and if he calls you again, say, 'Speak, Lord, your servant is listening.'" So Samuel went back to bed. 10 The Lord came and stood there, and called as he had before, "Samuel! Samuel!" Samuel answered, "Speak; your servant is listening." 1 Samuel 3:1-10

1 I urge you, then, I who am a prisoner because I serve the Lord: live a life that measures up to the standard God set when he called you. 2 Be always humble, gentle, and patient. Show your love by being tol-

erant with one another. 3 Do your best to preserve the unity which the Spirit gives by means of the peace that binds you together. 4 There is one body and one Spirit, just as there is one hope to which God has called you. 5 There is one Lord, one faith, one baptism; 6 there is one God and Father of all people, who is Lord of all, works through all, and is in all. 7 Each one of us has received a special gift in proportion to what Christ has given. 11 It was he who "gave gifts to people"; he appointed some to be apostles, others to be prophets, others to be evangelists, others to be pastors and teachers. 12 He did this to prepare all God's people for the work of Christian service, in order to build up the body of Christ. 13 And so we shall all come together to that oneness in our faith and in our knowledge of the Son of God; we shall become mature people, reaching to the very height of Christ's full stature. 14 Then we shall no longer be children, carried by the waves and blown about by every shifting wind of the teaching of deceitful people, who lead others into error by the tricks they invent. 15 Instead, by speaking the truth in a spirit of love, we must grow up in every way to Christ, who is the head. 16 Under his control all the different parts of the body fit together, and the whole body is held together by every joint with which it is provided. So when each separate part works as it should, the whole body grows and builds itself up through love. Ephesians 4:1-7; 11-16

43 The next day Jesus decided to go to Galilee. He found Philip and said to him, "Come with me!." 44 (Philip was from Bethsaida, the town where Andrew and Peter lived.) 45 Philip found Nathanael and told him, "We have found the one whom Moses wrote about in the book of the Law and whom the prophets also wrote about. He is Jesus son of Joseph, from Nazareth." 46 "Can anything good come from Nazareth?" Nathanael asked. "Come and see," answered Philip. 47 When Jesus saw Nathanael coming to him, he said about him, "Here is a real Israelite; there is nothing false in him!" 48 Nathanael asked him, "How do you know me?" Jesus answered, "I saw you when you were under the fig tree before Philip called you." 49 "Teacher," answered Nathanael, "you are the Son of God! You are the King of Israel!" 50 Jesus said, "Do you believe just because I told you I saw you when you were under the fig tree? You will see much greater things than this!" 51 And he said to them, "I am telling you the truth: you will see heaven open and God's angels going up and coming down on the Son of Man." John 1:43-51

From Isaiah, "Do not be afraid. I have redeemed you. I have called you by name. You are mine." Our lessons for today, all of them, speak in one way or another about that call of God to us. It is great to be called, great to be chosen. I remember when I was in second grade, I used to play inside with Philip Toftly and everybody else went outside for recess. He was a talented artist and I was always amazed at what he could draw on the blackboard. If I were a psychiatrist, I would have taken little Philip Toftly and made sure he had some good mental health care. But back then it was just interesting. The teacher warned me not to hang around with Philip all the time—and now I can see why. She told me to go out and play, so finally I did.

Teams were already chosen, so I just got on one. It was a kickball game. They were nice and said, "Jerstad, why don't you kick it once?" The objective was to get it across the goal way on the other side of the field. I ran, I kicked that baby, and, was it luck? Maybe even skill? Maybe my size elevens in second grade? That ball sprinted through everybody and landed in the goal, unbelievably. I was cheered! It was the last recess I ever spent inside. From then on, whenever they'd choose for kickball, it was "I get Jerstad." Oh, how great to be chosen!

My belief from reading the scriptures is that each one of us has been called and chosen by a heavenly Father. "I have redeemed you. I have called you by name. You are mine." That calling comes to us at our baptism, when he makes us his own. And he continues to call us through friends, through the word, through the fellowship of believers. "I have called you by name. You are mine."

To what does he call us? Our Epistle lesson tells us that, among other things, he calls us to a job, a life. Our Gospel lesson for today points out one aspect of that job. We are called, having received the Good News, to share it with others. We are called to be evangelists. We have Good News to share. And we're called to do it. We have here the little example of Philip, called by Christ. "Come with me." He, in turn, seeks out his friend Nathanael and says, "Come. We have found the one whom Moses wrote about."

Nathanael is a little skeptical about all of this. "Jesus came from Nazareth. What good can come out of Nazareth?" Philip could have gotten into an argument at this point and said, "Listen: I'm going to prove it to you." But all he says is, "Come and see." The invitation.

That is our calling, too—to be evangelists, to share. We do not have to be brilliant in terms of our knowledge of every existential, agnostic argument there is, counteracting it and coming forth with a strong, convincing proof at the end like a national debate champion.

I have a hunch that most people have not been brought to the Lord because of brilliant debate, but more because of personal testimony, quiet invitation. Each one of us can share that. Each one of us has a story to tell, but not in the old framework of "my life used to be terrible and now, I found the Lord, and life is great." In reality, it does not happen like that. If you read the Bible, Old Testament and New, you see that is not true. Struggle always happens along the way. But the reality of the presence of the Lord in our life, as he touches us, is something we can share—our brokenness and his grace.

A story tells of a famous nineteenth century agnostic, Huxley, who was at a country home. He was there with a number of people, and on Sunday morning most made preparation to go off to church.

He invited one man to stay home, and said to the man, "Please, would you just stay home and tell me why you believe?" The man was an old farmer who said, "Oh no, I'm going to church. I couldn't argue with you. You'd just destroy me."

Huxley said, "No, I don't want to argue. I just want to hear your story." So the old farmer stayed with him that Sunday morning and told him why he believed, and what the presence of the Lord meant in his life. The brilliant philosopher agnostic had tears in his eyes at the end of that little talk, and said, "I'd give my right arm if I could believe like you believe." There is more power in a simple, quiet testimony given to another than in some of the self-righteous sermons of the day.

We are called to be evangelical, to share the Good News. Our Old Testament lesson for today has three main characters: Samuel, an old priest named Eli, and God. Eli had not led a perfect life. His children were less than perfect. I am a preacher's kid, and sometimes preachers' kids are a little wild, but you should have seen those preacher's kids. Eli, imperfect in his position in the temple, sometimes abused his calling. But you have to give him credit for one thing. He was able to recognize in the experience of Samuel the call of the Lord.

Sometimes I feel like old Eli. There are days when it seems like my life is a shambles, and I feel like I'm not good for much. Somehow, God manages to pierce my shroud with his message: "I have called you. You are mine."

I invite you to listen. If your life has been in a turmoil, weighed down, or if, in the middle of the night you wake up worrying about your self-worth, or if you are just plain questioning the existence of God, listen to old Eli for a moment. "When it happens again, go back and lie down and say, 'Speak, Lord, for thy servant hears.'" For He is calling you, churning up the waters of your life. He has called you by name, you are His, and he has a task for you to do. Listen to him. Follow that call.

Be used by him to love the world, and pour yourself out to those around you. Challenge those things that are going on that are wrong. Consider what is spent on nuclear arms compared to what is spent on feeding hungry children. Think about taking care of the planet we live on. Listen to those who are hurting from addictions or who have lost a loved one.

Go lie down, be alone. Listen to the call. Don't be afraid. Don't worry. "I have redeemed you. I have called you by name. You are mine."

Reflection

The theme of this sermon resonates deeply with me. I was born to an unmarried woman, and back in those days, those pregnancies were kept a secret. The women were cloistered until they gave birth, and then the babies were taken away for adoption, and the women were told to go and live their lives and forget "this" happened.

I was one of those babies, removed from my birth mother right after I was born. But at six weeks old, I was chosen and adopted by George and Phoebe Skustad. They were forty and had adopted a six-month old boy three years earlier but wanted a girl to complete their little family. And that has made all the difference in my life.

When I was little my parents read a book to me about adoption, emphasizing that I was "chosen." This, along with the strong and secure love of my parents, made me feel unique, so, for many years, I had no interest in looking into my biological roots. Finally, at age 52, I felt a deep need to find out where I came from.

One of the reasons I had not searched earlier was that my adoptive mom had been devastated and left alone in life after my father died of a heart attack when he was 53. Shortly after that my brother was killed in a motorcycle accident while serving in the Navy. I was all she had left in terms of family. I knew it would disturb her to have me seeking another family.

So, after years of waiting for the right time and keeping her informed of every step I was taking, I began my search. I found out that my biological mother had died years earlier of her fifth heart attack, and my biological father had also died. But I did find two half-sisters in Minneapolis and introduced my mother to them.

When my daughter Rachel asked, "Grandma, does it bother you that mom is seeking her biological roots?"

She answered, "No, because she's mine, and that's that."

What a great line, what a great love, what a great memory!

God claims us for his own in the same way, no matter where our lives take us. We have been called. We were chosen. We belong. We are his.

The Chosen Children

Joy

In the same way, I tell you, there will be more joy in heaven over one sinner who repents than over ninety-nine respectable people who do not need to repent. When she finds it, she calls her friends and neighbors together, and says to them, "I am so happy I found the coin I lost. Let us celebrate!" Luke 15:7, 9

Think for a moment in your life about that time, that particular experience, that moment that has given you greatest joy—your number one. The most joyful moment you have experienced. What is it? What was it like? What was it like to be overwhelmed, captured, almost beyond yourself with that sense of joy?

Let me paint a few pictures of joy.

Number one: We lived for a time in Minneapolis, Minnesota, near Lake Nokomis. Lake Nokomis is noted for things like its muscle beach, little bikinis, and an all-summer-long hangout for convertibles, blankets, and fun and games.

However, when I think of Lake Nokomis, just blocks from my home, I think of one particular afternoon.

She was the most beautiful child I can ever remember. Her name was Julie. She had huge, deep brown eyes and blonde hair, almost like white cotton candy. Her skin tanned easily. She was a charmer from birth, my youngest sister.

She used to like to go down to Lake Nokomis with family and

friends, play in the sand, and paddle around in the water.

One day, when she was about six, she asked if I would take her to the lake. "Sure," I said, and we went. Once there I started checking out the chicks in their bikinis and suddenly realized I had lost track of my sister.

I looked around in a panic, but she was nowhere to be seen. I ran up and down the beach. I had her paged. She was nowhere. I called home—it was Saturday afternoon. My dad came down in the car, and the two of us split up, one on each side of the beach. We waded, hoping against hope we would not find a small body floating face down, but just not knowing.

Finally, in one last, desperate search, my dad ran down the beach. Ten minutes later I saw them coming through the crowd, daughter held snugly in her father's arms, both of them laughing through their tears. A moment of unutterable joy. The little lost sister was found.

Picture Number Two: I wish that we had a required reading list here at Augustana, and that you could not graduate until you had read at least a certain number of books. Definitely on that list would be *The Immense Journey* by Loren Eiseley, a brilliant, beautiful, poetic piece of work. Scientific, meditative, profoundly theological. A gift indeed.

In this writing, Loren Eiseley tells a story of his youth, when the university hired him to spend a summer capturing specific birds to be put into a large zoo for study and for display. He tells of coming to the barn late one evening.

He saw there was a hole in the top, and he knew it would be a natural nesting place for some kind of species of bird. With one hand he held his flashlight, and with the other he climbed up, and reached his hand in. He heard a sharp, shrill cry. He saw with his light that there were two birds, not one—sparrow hawks.

All of a sudden one of the pair screeched, went for his hand,

and hung on so that the other one might go free—his mate. She soared through the hole. He was able to capture the bird. His pride was hurt, he said, because of his wounds, but he carefully took the bird, and put it in a box. He decided to sleep in the barn.

The next morning, he got up, and was suddenly taken with the thought of the bird he had caught and decided to look at it again. Carefully he took it out of the box, held it in his hand, and said this:

A little breeze flowed over me again, and nearby a mountain aspen shook its tiny leaves. I suppose I must have had an idea then of what I was going to do, but I never let it come up into consciousness. I reached over and laid the hawk on the grass. He lay there a long minute without hope, unmoving, his eyes still fixed on that blue vault above him. It must have been that he was already so far away in heart that he never felt the release from my hand; he never even stood. He just lay with his breast against the grass. In the next second after that long minute, he was gone. Like a flicker of light, he had vanished with my eyes full on him but without even seeing a premonition of a wing beat. He was gone, straight into that towering emptiness of light and crystal that my eyes could scarcely bear to penetrate. For another long moment there was silence. I could not see him. The light was too intense. Then from far up somewhere a cry came ringing down. I was young then and had seen little of the world. But when I heard that cry, my heart turned over. It was not the cry of the hawk I had captured, for, by shifting my position against the sun, I was now seeing further up. Straight out of the sun's eye, where she must have been soaring restlessly above us for untold hours, hurtled his mate. And from far up, ringing from peak to peak of the summits over us, came a cry of such unutterable and ecstatic joy that it sounds down across the years and tingles among the cups on my quiet breakfast table.

Together again. A picture of joy. *"Consider the birds of the air,"* Jesus said. *"Your father in heaven cares for them, each one of them. How much more does he care for you?"*

There is the key. No matter what your experience of joy has been or will be, know that it is only a foretaste of that which is to come. For the true joy, the joy that lasts forever, is that joy which comes to us from our future, from the promise of him who loves us and gave his life for us, that penetrates our very present moment, that says, *"You are mine, your sins are forgiven."*

That joy rattles and sings across the mountain peaks of heaven, finds its way down into our hearts, buoys us up, and fills us, captures us, and then turns us loose, agents of that joy, that promise of his hope. Rejoice, because your names are written in the book of life.

Reflection

Who doesn't love a story with a happy ending? Thinking a small child who could not be located might be dead, and then finding her alive and safe is bound to provide unutterable joy, ecstatic joy. And Loren Eiseley's story about the sparrow hawk and his mate still makes me weep. How can some people think animals and birds do not have emotions?!

As I was typing Mark's questions at the beginning of this sermon, I had a hard time thinking of *moments* of joy. What came to me were times in our life together where it felt as if we were floating in joy—like when I found and fell in love with Mark. Although our relationship went through a few ups and downs before we were married, we were both head over heels in love as we started our life together as husband and wife.

Our marriage began in a makeshift grouping of rooms in the basement of Maude Goodrich's small apartment building. Sitting at our kitchen table for two, I could reach the stove, the sink and the refrigerator without getting up. The bedroom was wall-to-wall bed, a standard double. To reach the bathroom, we had to cross the hall and enter the laundry room. The shower was out the door and around the corner, located in the back of the small study. We were never sure what was going to crawl out of the drain.

It was a bargain, though, because our monthly rental bill, which included everything except our $5 phone bill, was $65. Since we were living on the wages we made as summer swim instructors, our low rent helped us get by. Mark left in the morning for classes, study, and work at Luther Seminary. I left for classes I was still taking at St. Olaf, and, later, for classes I was teaching in the Roseville school system. We looked forward to sharing stories at the end of the day.

To be that much in love, to have a husband who was also my

best friend, that was overpowering joy. I know it sounds uninteresting, but we both settled into marriage easily. Probably because I had been used to cooking, cleaning, and taking care of business since I was 13, and Mark had been pressed into duty at home with four younger sisters and had paid for his own education through multiple jobs, we easily slid into domestic life and were both ready for a family of our own.

We did, however, have our share of experiences that led to wishing our mate had come with an instruction manual. My mother taught me how to cook when I was young and always stressed nutritional meals. She was a strong believer in getting your iron through regular doses of liver. I sort of knew Mark did not like liver, but one evening I decided I could successfully camouflage it in a liver loaf. What was I thinking?!

I heard his footsteps come in the front door of the apartment, continue down the hall, and down the stairs toward our apartment. Usually a happy guy who greeted and hugged with enthusiasm, he silently went to the oven, took oven mitts, removed the pan of liver loaf, and quite ceremoniously carried it into the furnace room and dumped the whole thing, pan and all, into the incinerator. Message sent. Lesson learned.

Of course, I have had moments in life, also, moments when fear and anxiety melted into ecstatic joy. Professionally it was when my softball team won the NCAA Division II national tournament in Midland, Michigan, in 1991. Politically, it was when I won my first two elections to the South Dakota State Senate, in 2006 and 2008. But the personal life joys were far greater. Nothing could top the birth of each of our children. Rachel was our first baby, and we were excited and nervous.

My first birth experience was not a positive one. I was encouraged to take an epidural anesthetic, which was a new method of pain reduction in 1969. Long story short, there were mistakes made, I suffered all alone during the last hour of labor without anesthesia of any kind, and then they gave me such a large dose that I was paralyzed from the waist down. The baby had to be dragged out by forceps, while the doctors and nurses talked about who was with whom the night before.

So I refused an anesthetic for the next two births. Mike was born breach, but labor was fast. Our doctor in that small town was also our dear friend, so he allowed Mark to be with me, setting a new trend for Falls Hospital. Today, breach births are commonly done by C-section, but rarely so in the good old days.

The November morning Sarah was born dawned sunny, the first glimpse of sunlight in two weeks. As I lay writhing in pain, Mark was chatting away with the nurses, who had brought him coffee and toast. As my daughter Rachel would say, "Nice!" Fortunately, labor went quickly and soon our new daughter, Sarah, was draped across my stomach.

We both wanted children, but for me, having been born to a mother at a time when adoption laws sealed off any connection with blood relatives, it was a dream. The children were born close together, and I hoped that would make for close relationships. As they grew, they were good at sticking together, but there were certainly the normal disagreements and two-on-one naughty tricks, with Sarah usually the odd person out.

Time and shared experiences at our Rainy Lake cabin drew them together in a unique way. For several summers, a small, cozy cabin with no electricity, no warm water, and no phone service was our home for two months. The children's friends were each other.

I vacillated between being scared out of my wits at the isolation of the place (What if something happened to one of the kids at night and we were unable to navigate the dark lake sinister with rocks and reefs?) and loving the setting of sun-lit waters, pine branches swaying in the wind, a cozy fire in our split-rock fireplace.

A few Rainy Lake experiences escalated into terror, at least from my perspective, before extreme relief was transformed into joy. Rainy Lake, forty miles long and thirty miles wide, contains old rock formations, which lie stealthily just under the surface in hundreds of places. The bays stretch out to the horizon and sometimes beyond, inviting the wind to lift water into waves. And, of course, it rains. Our cabin sits serenely on the shore of Lost Bay, twelve miles east of the boat's mooring location at Rainy Lake Houseboats. The ride to and from the cabin is usually a peaceful twenty minutes on the water.

But not always. One Sunday afternoon we loaded the kids, ages three to seven, and some concrete, nails, and other building materials into our 19-foot open-bow tri-hull Sea Ray. We planned a run up to the cabin to deliver materials and look at the building progress and return, perhaps a two-hour trip. When we headed up to the cabin, the wind was blowing from the south, creating small, choppy waves as we followed the south shore. While we were getting ready to return, the wind suddenly shifted and picked up speed, clocking at 45 mph in some areas. Later we discovered there was a wind advisory with a warning to stay off the lake.

Not realizing the wind shift and velocity, we headed for home and met the wind and waves head on at the end of our little bay. Waves stood the front end almost straight up in the air and then sent us crashing down in the next instant, the spray cascading into the boat. Terrified, I had to pretend we were on a fun carnival ride, up and down, so the children would not panic. Mark kept the speed down and tried to work with the waves and the wind. Finally, after a grueling hour and a half, we arrived at the dock where we kept our boat. Relief became joy, and we celebrated with a family picnic. We had survived!

On another occasion, when the children were three, four and six, Mark decided it would be fun to commute to work from the cabin for a couple of weeks during our stay in International Falls. Of course, he left for work at 7 a.m. and returned in the evening, and I got to stay at the cabin with no phone or electricity and three small children.

The first day he generously took the old fishing boat with an ancient 16-horse power motor, telling me I would feel safer with the "big boat." During the gray, gloomy day, I was to keep a fire in the newly painted steel sauna stove to "burn the paint smell off." The kids accompanied me through the woods to the sauna to stoke the fire.

We had stepped inside the sauna for a few minutes when four-year-old Mike slipped and fell against the stove, burning his back. His screams of pain sent me into a panic. I quickly carried him to the lake and dunked him, then took him to the cabin to find ointment and bandages. It was a couple of hours before we both settled down. We read and played games until suppertime.

A thunderstorm in the early evening accentuated my fears at being alone and I was glad Mark would be back by 9 p.m. at the latest, after church.

It was 10 p.m. and no Mark. With darkness gathering, I loaded the kids, who now had their pajamas on, into the boat, and set out to look for him. When we got to the end of the bay, huge waves began crashing into the boat. In despair, I turned back, knowing Mark could never have navigated those waves in the fishing boat. We returned to the dock, and I put the kids to bed.

Feeling numb with fear and anxiety, I sat on the porch watching the cotton-like clouds stream past the front of the half moon. At 11:30 p.m., I heard the faint sound of a motor. Running to the dock, I saw him coming, slowly. Somehow he had managed to navigate the immense waves. "I was so scared, I started singing hymns," he told me. The motor was barely working, almost conking out as he entered Lost Bay. My emotions rendered me weak with relief, which eventually turned to joy. In between, I was angry about the chance he took with no life jacket.

We all have stories of times we were lost, or someone dear to us was missing, and then found, resulting in overwhelming joy, especially if the search has been long, hope is fading, and fear grips our hearts. I believe these experiences give us a hint, a premonition of the joy we will feel when we finally find that our names are truly written in the book of life, and that we, who were lost, now are found.

Forgiveness

8 But now you must get rid of all these things: anger, passion, and hateful feelings. No insults or obscene talk must ever come from your lips. Col. 3:8

26 If you become angry, do not let your anger lead you into sin, and do not stay angry all day. 27 Don't give the Devil a chance. 28 If you used to rob, you must stop robbing and start working, in order to earn an honest living for yourself and to be able to help the poor. 29 Do not use harmful words, but only helpful words, the kind that build up and provide what is needed, so that what you say will do good to those who hear you. 30 And do not make God's Holy Spirit sad; for the Spirit is God's mark of ownership on you, a guarantee that the Day will come when God will set you free. 31 Get rid of all bitterness, passion, and anger. No more shouting or insults, no more hateful feelings of any sort. 32 Instead, be kind and tenderhearted to one another, and forgive one another, as God has forgiven you through Christ. Ephesians 4:26-32

I'm a little bit frightened by it. Underneath the surface, the calm exterior that those of us who come from good, solid, Nordic stock have learned all so well to portray—that cool, calm, "quiet waters run deep" act that we're so easily tempted to slip into—seethes a restless, frustrated, powerful force. We call it anger. Some days I wish that you were all a bunch of hot-blooded Italians and would get those feelings out! But no, instead, we carry them inside, deep and strong and powerful.

What do I mean? Think about what happens in your bedroom. Your side is always so neat, and the other side looks like Hiroshima. And your roommate doesn't even know there is a difference! Day after week after month of this goes by. Slowly and quietly, you change, and finally in his or her ignorance your roommate says, "What's wrong?" Your big chance, and you say, "Oh, nothing." Inside, the acid runs hot. The power is there.

I think of so many married couples that I have counseled, and as we get into it, a sore spot is touched. And it starts to bubble. And simmer. And spill over like seeping sewer gas. Anger—frustration that boils—is savored, used. Keeping score, keeping track. Inside knowing, "I'm always better than the other." Feeling somehow wronged and letting it all churn. And on the outside, everything is just fine. Power resides in this feeling of anger and wrath.

A husband, frightened because of his wife who was consumed with rage, called me to their home once. I looked at her. Literally—I've never seen it before or since—the blood vessels in her eyes had burst and blood was coming out of her eyes. So much power in that anger and in that rage! There is power here, but the power that is actually here is not the eyes exploding. The power is in what it does to community, and what it does to us.

Frederick Buechner writes in a little book a beautiful, poignant, perceptive paragraph: "Of the seven deadly sins, anger is possibly the most fun. To lick your wounds, to smack your lips over grievances long past, to roll over your tongue the prospect of bitter confrontations still to come, to savor to the last toothsome morsel both the pain you are given and the pain you are giving back. In many ways, it is a feast fit for a king. The chief drawback is that what you are wolfing down is yourself. The skeleton at the feast is you." There is power here—anger unresolved, savored, turned outward, destroys community. Anger unresolved, savored, turned inward, destroys you. We call it depression.

I recently read of an Episcopal priest who, after 21 years in the priesthood, finally collapsed—a nervous breakdown. In an interview, he said, "My chief problem was that I was never able to deal with anger. I stuffed it, kept it inside, and it ate me up from the inside out." Anger in and of itself is not wrong. The Bible never says that anger is wrong. Do you think Jesus was not angry when he walked through the temple and started tipping over tables and pushing people aside and letting animals run loose? He was angry, of course!

The Bible tells us, "Don't let the sun go down on your anger." Deal with it at the time it occurs. Don't stuff it. Don't think that by keeping it inside everything is going to be fine. Effectively, appropriately, at the right time, deal with those feelings, and in so doing community is not destroyed, but community is created.

What was it that Jesus said again? If you come before the altar and realize that someone has something against you, or you have something against someone, stop—even if it is right in the middle of the Creed—quit, leave everything right there, take off. Go and find that person. Resolve the conflict. Let peace be created. Then come back. Then, by the way, you will have something indeed to be thankful for. Paul said it, "Get rid of all bitterness, passion and anger." Do not store it up. Never let it get out of control. Get rid of it! *"No more shouting or insults, no more hateful feelings of any sort."* And here is the key: *"Instead, be kind and tender-hearted to one another, and forgive one another, as God has forgiven you in Christ."*

Late last night, Sandy had worked hard out in the garage (and it was cold out there) stripping an old, beautiful walnut table. It was perfect. This morning she said to me, "Mark, will you help me carry it down to the basement, so I can finish it up?"

I said, "I'll be happy to."

As I was carrying it, I didn't notice this great big screw sticking out of one side of the door. I squeezed the table through, and there, all of a sudden, I almost printed the word "gouge" in the walnut.

Sandy looked at me, and the words in her eyes were not, "Oh, how interesting. I always wanted this table to have that distressed look." There was a flash—I'd seen it before—and I thought, "Oh-oh, what's going to happen now?"

We carried the table back out to the garage, where, I figured, she would fix it later. Then we drove in stoney silence to my office. All of a sudden, as she pulled up to drop me off, her hand reached over to mine. A smile spread across her face indicating love and peace in her heart. She was forgiveness personified. Once again in the Jerstad household there was community, and there was love.

There is power, phenomenal power in anger and in rage. But, my friends, there is so much more power in forgiveness and in love in the name of our Lord Jesus Christ. That power, that forgiveness, that love, is for you. Share it!

Reflection

Mark was big on forgiveness. Holding onto a grudge was not usually part of his nature. He was a master at reading people, and knew intuitively when people were not owning up to their feelings. Our son Mike inherited this ability from his father, and I found I could never hide my feelings from him.

Mark would get angry once in awhile, and, when he did, he usually stuck his finger in his mouth and bit down on it. That was the sign to us in the family that he was extremely unhappy with something that had happened. However, he was usually the first to talk things out and to forgive or ask for forgiveness.

Sometimes, however, when the tables were turned, it took a

little time and nudging. We were living in International Falls where Mark was the pastor of Zion Lutheran Church. I was seven months pregnant with our third child, and it was an unusually hot night in September. We had no air conditioning in our house, because, why would you if you lived in the icebox of the nation?

We were trying to get to sleep, and neither of us had anything on. Restless, I got up to adjust the shade so the street light would not hit me in the eye. At the moment, when my pregnant, naked form was framed in the window as I reached for the shade, my husband thought it would be amusing to switch the light on.

In panic, I dropped my pregnant body to the floor. Now he was thoroughly entertained. He laughed and laughed. And could not stop laughing. Just when I thought he was done, he would burst out with another snort of laughter. Finally I went into the kids' bedroom to try to get some rest.

In the morning, when he came down for breakfast, he was still snickering, but trying hard to ask for some serious forgiveness. I, of course, granted him my forgiveness, but not until he apologized profusely.

It reminds me of the time he got the giggles in church. When he had not had much sleep, he was more prone to uncontrollable laughter. He was chanting the liturgy when the church organist landed on a particularly off-tune chord. He let a little snicker escape from his lips, then turned and said to the congregation, "You know, I have always worried that one day I would get the giggles in church, and, you know what, I think today is the day." With that, he burst into uncontrollable laughter, which went on for some time. Before long, there was a giggle over there, a snort here, and the whole congregation joined in. It took him two tries before he could get himself and the rest of the people under control. No one seemed to need him to ask for forgiveness, as they reveled in the best belly laugh they had had for a long time.

These incidents in our past are light-hearted examples of forgiveness, silly stories we enjoyed telling. But there are many examples of forgiveness that are almost unfathomable. One of the most profound examples of forgiveness I can think of is when the Amish people forgave the shooter, Charles Roberts, who killed five of their daughters and wounded five others in a shooting rampage at an Amish school in Lancaster, PA, in 2006.

In an article entitled "Amish Grace and Forgiveness," the following excerpt describes what happened.

"It's ironic that the killer was tormented for nine years by the premature death of his young daughter. He never forgave God for her death. Yet, after he cold-bloodedly shot 10 innocent Amish school girls, the Amish almost immediately forgave him and showed compassion toward his family."

I know I have a ways to go before I could emulate that depth of forgiveness. Where do the Amish get such faith and behavior? They follow Jesus' teaching, which is rich with admonitions to forgive one another.

We have a choice: hold onto anger and feelings of revenge, and live a bitter and perhaps vengeful life; or choose the path of forgiveness and let God direct us as we move toward a love-filled life of grace.

After all, we are all guilty of a multitude of sins, yet God gave his own son to wipe out all our transgressions, big and little. How can we ever think of holding onto our anger and not forgiving our brother or sister?!

Gratitude: A Matter of Perspective

1 Therefore, since we are justified by faith, we have peace with God through our Lord Jesus Christ. 2 Through him we have obtained access to this grace in which we stand, and we rejoice in our hope of sharing the glory of God. 3 More than that, we rejoice in our sufferings, knowing that suffering produces endurance, 4 and endurance produces character, and character produces hope, 5 and hope does not disappoint us, because God's love has been poured into our hearts through the Holy Spirit which has been given to us. 6 While we were still weak, at the right time Christ died for the ungodly. 7 Why, one will hardly die for a righteous man—though perhaps for a good man one will dare even to die. 8 But God shows his love for us in that while we were yet sinners Christ died for us. Romans 5: 1-8 (RSV)

33 Who will accuse God's chosen people? God himself declares them not guilty! 34 Who, then, will condemn them? Not Christ Jesus, who died, or rather, who was raised to life and is at the right side of God, pleading with him for us! 35 Who, then, can separate us from the love of Christ? Can trouble do it, or hardship or persecution or hunger or poverty or danger or death? 36 As the scripture says, "For your sake we are in danger of death at all times; we are treated like sheep that are going to be slaughtered." 37 No, in all these things we have complete victory through him who loved us! 38 For I am certain that nothing can separate us from his love: neither death nor life, neither angels nor other heavenly rulers or powers, neither the present nor the future, 39 neither the world above nor the world below—there is nothing in all creation that will ever be able to separate us from the love of God which is ours through Christ Jesus our Lord. Romans 8:31-39

Reflect with me about our fundamental attitude toward life, the one that shapes much of our outlook and behavior. So many of us, myself included, take the good things that happen to us completely for granted, as if we richly deserve all the gifts God showers upon us. We placidly drift through each day unthinkingly accepting our good fortune, without thanksgiving, without gratitude. We confess every Sunday that God loves us and that Jesus died for us, but without seriously meditating on the miracle of God's love and living our lives overflowing with gratitude.

The consequences of this attitude can be disastrous and tragic. When things don't go well, we become mired in self-pity. We complain that God has deserted us and no longer cares, or worse, we conclude that God does not exist. We feel that no one appreciates us, despite our many attractive qualities. We have done so much for so many people, all of whom selfishly refuse to reciprocate with a little esteem, gratitude, and attention to our needs. As a result of such brooding, we can become negative and bitter, turning in upon ourselves rather than toward God in repentance. Indeed, often we are in no condition to accept God's help when offered, or even to want it, since we would rather be left alone with wounded ego and a martyr's complex and without self-esteem. Our whole world is centered on ourselves.

How radically different Paul's attitude is: *"Not only so, but we also rejoice in our sufferings."* Rejoice in suffering! This sentiment sounds so strange these days, yet it was a constant refrain in the New Testament and was so characteristic of the first Christians that their joy and love in the face of terrible suffering conquered the Roman world. I believe the key to their attitude, the cure for self-pity, and one of the chief foundations of the Christian life is the virtue of gratitude.

There is a form of gratitude that Christians share with many others: the gratitude for health, food, clothing, our loved ones, and other good things in life. There is nothing at all wrong with this; we should thank God for the blessings we receive each day. In fact, most of us fall far short even on this account. How many of us truly live each day full of gratitude for these basic necessities? Imagine how such thankfulness alone would transform our lives. Yet this is not the gratitude I wish to emphasize. It is not the most fundamental and Christian form of gratitude, and, ultimately, it will not sustain us in times of severe trial when, like Job, we lose all the material benefits of this life. It is not the gratitude Paul is expressing in these passages.

The uniquely Christian form of gratitude—the gratitude that transforms lives—arises from our failure, our slavery to sin (whose wage truly is death), and our desperate need for God. It is an extraordinary fact that while we were yet God's enemies, he still loved us! Although most of us will scarcely risk our wealth or security in the aid of anyone, God has sacrificed his own Son for the sake of his enemies. And by such unmerited love and grace we are saved from ourselves, with his wounds we are indeed healed. Best of all, nothing—not hardship, persecution, famine, death, or anything else in the universe—can separate us from God's love in Christ Jesus.

This love and sacrifice is incredible, miraculous, totally and absolutely undeserved. When the real situation—our abject failure, sin, and need—is truly understood, the only conceivable Christian response to God's sacrificial love on the cross is overwhelming and boundless gratitude: gratitude, not in response to material blessings at all, but gratitude in response to unmerited, unconditional, and unlimited love. *"We love because he first loved us"* (1 John 4:19). There is no way of repaying God, no way of retiring our debt because it is infinite. The only adequate response is love and gratitude—as the hymn says, "Love so amazing, so divine, demands my soul, my life, my all."

Strangely enough, it really is in losing our life out of gratitude for God's love that we actually save it. When we live continually filled with gratitude to God for our salvation, we are liberated from self-centeredness and excessive concern with material possessions; we avoid the swamp of self-pity; and we are led to repentance, joyful obedience, and a new life. Since our whole perspective on existence has been radically transformed, we can live each day like the lilies of the field, unburdened by anxiety and excessive preoccupation with ourselves.

Because the Creator of the universe loves us enough to sacrifice his own Son and number the very hairs on our head, we are important, and life has ultimate meaning despite the fact that we may be called to suffer great hardship and even die in His service. From this perspective, many of life's little troubles and aggravations, which often embitter our days and darken our mood, are seen to be trivial and insignificant. Such gratitude truly does give a joy that cannot be taken away by times of pain and suffering. It empowers us to selflessly serve God and others (even our enemies) in love, and under girds hope in the ultimate meaning of life and the eventual triumph of Good. The overpowering gratitude for his own salvation, I believe, empowered Luther throughout his life and underlay the sentiments expressed in his greatest hymn:

God's Word forever shall abide, no thanks to foes
   who fear it;
For God himself fights by our side with weapons of
   the Spirit.
If they take our house, goods, fame, child, or spouse,
Wrench our life away, they cannot win the day.
The Kingdom's ours forever!

In another letter (1 Cor. 13:13), Paul exclaims that faith, hope and love will always remain, with love being the greatest of all. True indeed! But intertwined with these three supreme virtues, like golden threads in the embroidery of the Christian life, is gratitude—a virtue arising from faith and sustaining hope, humility, and love. Let us beseech God to give us genuine, profound gratitude for the gift of his own Son so that our lives may be transformed by his love, and we may be made instruments of his peace.

Reflection

I have never known a person who was more in love with life, at ease with himself, and grateful for every day than Mark. One of my favorite times of the day was early morning when Mark was getting dressed, excited for whatever the day might bring, and usually whistling or singing. His exuberance filled our house. He expressed his gratitude for life in his genuine love and appreciation of others, whether he knew them or not.

On one occasion, he got a phone call from someone trying to sell something on the phone. Instead of quickly getting rid of the person, he started gently asking him about his job and his life. When he asked him if he liked his job, the man's reply was, "I'd rather be chewing razor blades." Mark sympathized with him and listened a bit longer to his unhappiness before letting him go.

Because he cared about people regardless of who they were, his ministry to others elicited gratitude. While we lived in International Falls, he often received calls in the middle of the night from a nurse at the hospital. Someone was dying. Could he please come? Never mind if he knew him or her or not or if that person belonged to his church. Many in "the Falls" knew of his care and compassion and ability to minister to those in crisis. He was literally "on call" 24-7 during our years there.

One night he got a call about midnight from the mortuary. A young man had been killed in a car accident, an apparent suicide. Mark was asked to find his estranged wife and tell her. So he went to the Border Bar, and, as he walked in, the band stopped playing, and the crowd fell silent. When he found the woman, he tried to talk her into stepping outside with him, so he could tell her about her husband. When she refused to leave, he shared the news right there and caught her in his arms as she fell. With that, he reported, it was easy to get her outside. He simply scooped her up and carried her outside and laid her on the grass. When she came to, he tenderly ministered to her grief and feelings of great guilt.

Some psychologists contend that the opposite of revenge is gratitude, and that the former is ultimately destructive in a person's life, while the latter is the most powerful positive emotion one can experience. I had a sea change in my life right after Mark died. A feeling of peacefulness and gratitude came over me, and, for the most part, my anxieties and worries vanished. In one way, it was as if Mark handed off his sense of peace and trust to me as he faced death. I have felt this peacefulness ever since, even through the years I spent grieving. Whatever the source, I am grateful.

In addition, I feel an immense gratitude for: my adoptive parents; my marriage to Mark; my children and my grandchildren; health and strength for each day; friends; meaningful work to do; and, above all, for my faith.

I am also grateful for my life, which hung in the balance when I was 15.

It was a gorgeous fall day in southern Minnesota, with the sky a deep, brilliant blue. My mother and I were visiting my Aunt Julie and Uncle Marvin (my father's brother) on their farm, where my father had grown up. It was Minnesota Education Association meeting week, so I was out of school for four days and my mother and I decided it would be a good time to visit the only extended family we had on their farm near Grand Meadow. I loved the farm and I loved horses.

My young cousin, Jane, and I had been riding that afternoon, and as the shadows started to lengthen, it was time to put the horse away in the barn. My horse was a gentle mare that my uncle had bought from a Girl Scout camp. But that day as I was encouraging the horse toward the barn, something went wrong, and the horse whirled on me and let fly with both rear hooves, striking me square in the stomach with one of the hooves.

It happened so fast I didn't see it coming, but suddenly I was flying backwards through the air with a horrendous pain in my stomach. I landed on my back, unable to breathe and in agony.

My uncle saw the accident happen from the house, but was unable to do a thing to prevent it. He ran over to see how I was, and began consoling me and encouraging me. He said when he was young he was running to the house from the barn and tripped over a cultivator and broke two ribs. He said he still went to the dance that night.

He told me he would pull the car over and take me in to the doctor. It was only four miles to town, but it wasn't long before both sitting up and lying down caused excruciating pain. My uncle stopped by his sister's house in town to pick up my mother, who was having coffee there. Terrified, she jumped into the car with us.

When we got to the doctor's office just around the corner, I stumbled out of the car and into the office. I was taken to the examining room, where the doctor did some probing and then wanted to take an X-ray. As I was standing up in front of the machine, the world started spinning. "I'm going to faint," I stammered. The last thing I heard was my mother telling me not to.

When I woke up, I was on an ambulance cart, ready to be loaded into the ambulance that also doubled as a hearse for that small town. The doctor told me he was sending me to Rochester, and that I probably had a ruptured spleen. He gave me a shot to help with the pain, and all I remember was the siren wailing as we went through several small towns on the way to Rochester. Upon arrival, the attending doctor, after much poking, probing, and pushing, told me they were going to make a small incision and sew up a small tear in my liver.

The small tear turned out to be a gash the length of my liver and an inch deep. The best abdominal surgeon was called in, and my mother was told not to leave the hospital. I was given eight pints of blood to replace the seven I lost. Later on the doctors would tell me that I had had a one in ten chance of arriving at the hospital alive and a one in 100 chance of pulling through the surgery.

Grateful for my caregivers and my visitors in the days that followed, I vowed I would always visit or send cards to people I knew who were in the hospital. The odds were so stacked against me that even Dr. Charles Mayo (the son of one of the founding doctors) came to see this miracle of healing. My faith tells me God was right there every minute, helping my body, the doctors, and the nurses, as I was kept alive and healed with only a sizeable right angle scar on my stomach as a reminder of my scrape with death.

I related this story to my granddaughter, Elizabeth, one day, stating that she would never have been born if I had not lived. She pondered that for a few seconds, then announced that she would have, because her mother would have had babies anyway. I had to laugh at the sheer optimism and uniqueness of her perspective. Oh, to think like a child!

Table Talk

14 When the hour came, Jesus took his place at the table with the apostles. 15 He said to them, "I have wanted so much to eat this Passover meal with you before I suffer! 16 For I tell you, I will never eat it until it is given its full meaning in the Kingdom of God." 17 Then Jesus took a cup, gave thanks to God, and said, "Take this and share it among yourselves. 18 I tell you that from now on I will not drink this wine until the Kingdom of God comes." 19 Then he took a piece of bread, gave thanks to God, broke it, and gave it to them, saying, "This is my body, which is given for you. Do this in memory of me." 20 In the same way, he gave them the cup after the supper, saying, "This cup is God's new covenant sealed with my blood, which is poured out for you." Luke 22:14-20

The Lord is my shepherd, I shall not want. He makes me lie down in green pastures; he leads me beside still waters; he restores my soul. He leads me in right paths for his name's sake. Even though I walk through the darkest valley, I fear no evil; for you are with me; your rod and your staff—they comfort me. You prepare a table before me in the presence of my enemies; you anoint my head with oil; my cup overflows. Surely goodness and mercy shall follow me all the days of my life, and I shall dwell in the house of the Lord my whole life long. Psalm 23, RSV

She presides over our dining room like a well-loved grandmother. She is round but can expand to accommodate many. Refinished by Sandy, her solid oak is golden in hue and her patina retains the scars of age. One can only fantasize with delight about her early history, but she emerged from her *urgeschichte* into our lives back in 1953 when she began a 25-year stint at my wife's family cabin on beautiful Lake Vermillion.

Upon our move to Sioux Falls, she was promoted to the dining room and has been most gracious and inviting in her new position. During the day, she becomes the repository for mail, school papers, books, and the place for paying bills, doing homework, coloring and playing games.

But she is at her best when she puts on her batik place mats and handmade pottery, or her three-generation-old hand-created lace and century old Bavarian china, rimmed in wide bands of cobalt blue and well-leafed with gold. Lit with candles, she graciously feeds family and friends, takes part in intimate conversations and warm laughter, post-meal devotions and prayer.

Around this table, you do more than consume food. Something happens. This experience happens as though you are embraced by a loving grandmother. You get sung to, rocked, snuggled, bounced, tickled, and loved. You experience community.

If the tables of our lives could talk, I suspect they could tell us much about ourselves. Perhaps they might tell us about relationships and love gone cold like the food barely touched and left on the plate. Or they might tell us about angry words hissed out like the scorching steam from the teapot on the stove. Maybe they would tell us about meals hurriedly eaten in shifts, each member of the family too involved in his or her own life to be concerned about creating community. Our tables could tell us about the pain of eating alone, a marriage broken by divorce or death.

Or maybe our tables would tell us about our excesses in food and drink. Isaiah said it: *"The prophets are too drunk to understand the visions that God sends, and the priests are too drunk to decide the cases that are brought to them. The tables where they sit are all covered by vomit, and not a clean spot is left."* We drink too much and eat too much. We consume, and consume, and we are not concerned about those who have nothing.

I wonder what the tables in our community could tell us about those among us who sit alone meal after meal, craving companionship but not feeling accepted as part of our community. I wonder what the tables of the world might tell us about our brothers and sisters who have little, who do not have to discipline themselves not to eat, but are concerned with survival. The pains in their stomachs are not from stuffing themselves, but from simple hunger. If the tables of our lives could talk, they could tell us much.

Jesus gave high priority to the table during his life on earth. For him, it was a place of community. At the table where he presided, all were welcome. Of Jesus it was said, "He receives sinners and eats with them." At table with Jesus there was joy. Witness the party at the home of Zacheaus.

At table with Jesus there was forgiveness. Just ask the woman who washed his feet with her tears. At table with Jesus there was always thanks to the Father: *"...he took bread and after he had given thanks..."*

Jesus used the table in his stories, sometimes as a place of judgment: the rich man who feasted sumptuously and the beggar Lazarus who did not even get the scraps. Jesus loved to tell about the feast to come, the table of the kingdom, the great banquet to celebrate the victory, to share in the community of love without end.

And Jesus gave us a down payment, a symbol of what that table can be for us now. It is the table of communion, the table where all are invited, because Jesus is both host and the host—the meal. It is the table where community is created and celebrated. It is the table where excess is forbidden, but where there is enough, always, for all.

At this table there is forgiveness, hope, and strength. We find peace in the midst of a sometimes-frantic life at this table, a table that binds us with all people and impels us to do something about the hunger of our brothers and sisters. Finally, at this table, we celebrate with happy anticipation the heavenly feast of love.

Let our tables, whether here or at home or in a restaurant be places of thanksgiving, where we confess our dependence on God for all that we have. Let them be places of community, where we take time to get to know one another better. Let them be places of respite and calm in the storm: "You prepare a table before me in the presence of my enemies;" a place of love, of worship, of laughter, of joy.

Let our tables be reminders of those who have less than we have and let us be inspired to turn this concern into acts of generosity. Let them be a place where all are invited, where we reach out beyond ourselves, for, as Jesus said, "Inasmuch as you have done it to the least of these my brothers and sisters, you have done it to me."

Sandy's mother, Phoebe, Rachel, Mark, Mike and Sarah

Reflection

I smile, remembering.

That table has been part of my life since I was five or six and my parents bought a little cabin on Big Bay of Lake Vermillion. The table was left along with some other furniture, including a big old wood cook stove in the little kitchen. We used the cabin spring, summer, and fall, and usually made a trip or two up there in the winter, skiing in the quarter mile from the main road.

The table was often made larger with the sturdy oak leaves and hosted bowls and platters of food—mashed potatoes, freshly caught walleye, fresh bread and sweet corn. I remember eating until my sides ached. I was always an active person, especially as a kid, so running off those calories was never a problem. Beyond that, I was growing. The table was also full of happy, talkative people, friends of my parents mainly.

In the evening came the card games, or just sitting and talking, followed by some yummy dessert. After my father died, my mother and I used to go to the cabin, but not as often. It seemed lonesome with just the two of us. But we still sat down to eat at that same table, and usually played cards together in the evening.

Mark and I bought the cabin from my mom a few years before we moved to Sioux Falls. When we sold the cabin, we made certain the table was not part of the deal. It was loaded up with care and came with us. I refinished it, bringing out the rich honey oak color, and the table became a part of our everyday life, as Mark reported.

One of my favorite memories was of a Christmas when the children were in elementary school. I had prepared a special dinner that included fondue with hot oil for cooking small pieces of meat and vegetables. The red and green colors on the table were softly muted by candlelight. Christmas music played in the background.

What happened next was at first a little frightening, then

amusing. Sarah managed somehow to tip the fondue pot, so some of the oil spilled onto the table and it also capsized a candle, which in turn lit the oil on fire. Everyone screamed. I raced to the kitchen for a wet towel. Once it was established that no one had been hurt and the house was not in danger of burning down, first smothered and then uncontrollable laughter erupted.

That table still serves as the setting used most often for food and fellowship in my home, now mainly inhabited by one person and two cats. Often littered with projects or papers to be corrected, it also welcomes family and friends together for meals and conversation. My heart is warmed by all the memories of laughter and love. Just gazing at the scarred wood warms my heart, filling it with gratitude for nourishment taken in and love shared.

During the day, my grandchildren like to do art projects at the table. One day Elizabeth used indelible ink and left permanent marks. Wide-eyed with horror, she looked at me.

"It's OK," I said. "It just makes it more memorable." During the evening, our favorite family games, "Rook" and "Taboo" may appear. Mike and Kelly are always victorious at "Taboo," no matter who opposes them. It's not fair. They finish each other's sentences all the time.

What an apt metaphor Mark used to illustrate God's gracious love to us, providing us with daily food for our bodies. But much more important, it illustrated our invitation to a table spread for all, where we partake of a real feast, God's body and blood, uniting us to him in faith forever.

In 1979, we heard of the killing fields of Cambodia, of the millions of Cambodians who had been murdered or displaced. Mark asked his student congregation at Augustana if they would like to help by hosting two couples, one with a small child. The answer was a resounding, "Yes!"

Arrangements were made through Lutheran Social Services

with First Lutheran Church also helping out. We were able to involve our children in helping prepare the small house located on 33rd Street, the spot where the softball team now has an outdoor batting cage. We cleaned and painted and helped furnish the small home, which housed the two Chau families.

As we continued providing whatever assistance we could, including helping to tutor them in English, we became a part of a circle of love provided to us and others by our new Cambodian friends. Each time we visited, we were seated in a comfortable chair and provided a drink and food. Their hospitality overflowed, and we were brought into their home and family through the sharing of a small meal. A continuing cycle of sharing. A sacred event.

They did not have a round oak table, but the love and sharing and reaching out was still there. We who sought to help and share something with them were given the treasure of friendship and generosity, which exists to this very day.

Not long ago, I slid into a chair at one of the Chinese restaurants our immigrant friends have worked hard to establish. A smiling face welcomed me and cool water refreshed me. Soon the table was filed with my favorite dishes—without my having to ask.

As a good waiter knows without being asked, as mothers know before their children beg, as hostesses anticipate the needs of their guests, so God calls us to the table knowing what we need, calls us to divine nourishment and love, and then welcomes us all.

Roadblocks to Faith

19 It was late that Sunday evening, and the disciples were gathered together behind locked doors, because they were afraid of the Jewish authorities. Then Jesus came and stood among them. "Peace be with you," he said. 20 After saying this, he showed them his hands and his side. The disciples were filled with joy at seeing the Lord. 21 Jesus said to them again, "Peace be with you. As the Father sent me, so I send you." 22 Then he breathed on them and said, "Receive the Holy Spirit. 23 If you forgive people's sins, they are forgiven; if you do not forgive them, they are not forgiven." 24 One of the twelve disciples, Thomas (called the Twin), was not with them when Jesus came. 25 So the other disciples told him, "We have seen the Lord!" Thomas said to them, "Unless I see the scars of the nails in his hands and put my finger on those scars and my hand in his side, I will not believe." 26 A week later the disciples were together again indoors, and Thomas was with them. The doors were locked, but Jesus came and stood among them and said, "Peace be with you." 27 Then he said to Thomas, "Put your finger here, and look at my hands; then reach out your hand and put it in my side. Stop your doubting, and believe!" 28 Thomas answered him, "My Lord and my God!" 29 Jesus said to him, "Do you believe because you see me? How happy are those who believe without seeing me!" 30 In his disciples' presence Jesus performed many other miracles which are not written down in this book. 31 But these have been written in order that you may believe that Jesus is the

Messiah, the Son of God, and that through your faith in him you may have life. John 20:19-31

Lord knows, we all would like to believe; I mean really believe. Each of us would like to have, to be given, a faith that is strong, sturdy, powerful, rich, and full. Lord knows there isn't one of us that would not like to be captured by something that helps us to see things in a new way, to be almost possessed by a power greater and beyond ourselves, and to understand everything in a new light.

Augustine said, "Thou hast created us for thyself and we are restless until we find our peace in thee." We would like to find the peace that bubbles up from a rich, powerful, total kind of faith. Søren Kierkegaard said, "Purity of heart is to will one thing." Who of us has a pure heart? Often it seems like our life is in pieces, fractured, in a thousand little bits all over the place. We are hungry to believe.

Joe Sittler tells one of my favorite stories. After he gave a lecture about the Christian faith in simple terms, one of his brilliant graduate students walked out of class and said, under his breath, "If it were true, t'would do." The Lord knows how we would really like to believe.

At times we all distance ourselves from the Lord and the Church, but show up at church once in a while anyway, just on the chance the Spirit will settle on us and cause us to believe. We keep hoping there is more to life than the everyday grind.

Even though we hope and wait for faith, there are some strong and real roadblocks to faith. We know them all too well. Today's Gospel speaks of those roadblocks. We see the disciples gathered together behind locked doors. What unites them is fear, a common roadblock for all of us. We know what it feels like to be afraid, and we know what fear does to us.

We are afraid to really believe, because if we do maybe that belief is going to carve our life in a totally different way from the nice, neat package that we have laid out for ourselves. We're afraid to risk, because we're afraid of failure. We trudge along, doing all the things that we know are safe, and living a well-ordered little life.

Often we are afraid of death, and young or old we contemplate it, and what our end means. Sometimes it seems to leap up and grab us, especially late at night, and the fear is almost literally paralyzing. We hear that silken whisper from the dark side of our life that haunts us with the idea that all of life is meaningless, and, when we die, that is the end. We are afraid, and that fear of life and fear of death becomes a roadblock to our faith.

As Jesus stepped into their midst on that first Easter Sunday and spoke with them about sins, he understood another of the roadblocks to faith: guilt. It is one of our major roadblocks as well. Maybe for one of us it is that "big sin," that one experience in our past that we drag along with us every single day of our life. We could tell a tale or two about what guilt does, about how it can paralyze our lives and squeeze the joy from us.

Our sins and our guilt take our focus away from the gift of God and God's love and forgiveness in our lives. In addition, we tend to rationalize our actions. "Well, everybody sins, and it's God's job to forgive, and besides, I live in grace, so it makes no difference what I do," is the way we too often think. We tend to have a kind of separation between our life and ourselves, and we live in what Bonhoeffer calls, "cheap grace." We take God's forgiveness for granted, we take God for granted, and the life of sin becomes a roadblock for us.

Another roadblock, the reality of doubt, is personified by Thomas in our text for today. "Unless I get my hands in his wound and I see him face to face, I will not believe." We know doubt in many forms. Is there one of us who has not struggled with the reality of our Christian faith? The rational part of our mind wonders if faith is just pure psychological wish fulfillment, that from the dawn of time people needed to find out an answer to the reason for our being and have created a power greater than ourselves to be the answer to our questions.

I'm not talking about the kind of doubt that Paul Tillich talks about, that doubt that is a part of our faith. As our Lord said, we walk by faith, not by sight. The other side of the coin of faith is doubt. Faith implies not knowing for sure. If we knew, it would be sight. I'm not talking about that rich kind of doubt that spurs us to struggle and to grow and mature. That kind of doubt is in essence a gift of our Lord, which causes us to take a closer look at our life, and ask vital, life struggle questions.

The kind of doubt that is a roadblock to faith is the kind of doubt that can paralyze us, that can harden us, that can turn us away from God. It is a destructive doubt.

To the disciples, who were beleaguered with all of these roadblocks to faith, Jesus appeared. He simply appeared to the men who were hiding behind locked doors, full of fear, doubt, and guilt. They were afraid of the Jews, of what might happen, and of what already had happened. Uninvited, Jesus showed up. They had not prayed for him to come, but he came anyway.

Fear could not keep him away, guilt could not keep him away, closed doors could not keep him away. He just showed up. The risen Christ was there for his disciples, as he is here today for us. The call of the Gospel is a call to open up our eyes again, to see Jesus when he shows up in our lives. He has never been absent. We have closed our eyes to him.

When this happens, things change. Our Gospel text tells us that those disciples who were afraid were suddenly overjoyed when they saw the Lord. This kind of joy, deep and profound, can visit a person even in the most trying times. Some of the most brilliant witnesses to this are survivors of the holocaust, who have talked about the deep joy they experienced, living literally in hell, when they felt the presence of the Lord among them.

Our Gospel text says, *"He breathed on them and said, 'Receive the Holy Spirit.'"* Jesus brings and gives the gift of the Holy Spirit to us, to each of us. This gift is profound, and often misunderstood. We have often trivialized the Holy Spirit by locking him into the gift of speaking in tongues or the raising of hands in prayer or faith healing. The gift of the Holy Spirit is God present with us.

Jesus announced that, even though he had to return to the Father, he would leave his Spirit with us. That spirit ignites faith in our hearts. As Luther said, "I believe that I cannot by my own reason or strength believe in Jesus Christ my Lord, or come to him, but the Holy Spirit has called me through the Gospel." God's spirit shows up and overcomes fear, guilt, and doubt to help us believe. Through him fear is replaced by joy, guilt is replaced by forgiveness. Through him doubt is replaced by hope. God gave his disciples his Holy Spirit, and they were overjoyed.

In light of today's text, we may feel restless. We would like the kind of faith that burns within us. Where do we go? To whom do we turn?

Listen: *"But these have been written in order that you may believe that Jesus is the Messiah, the Son of God, and that through your faith in him you may have life."* This message drives us back to his word, to his promise, and there, struggling again with that word, we will hear that we are loved, that we are forgiven, that we are not abandoned. We will hear that there is hope for us in this life and beyond this life, and we will hear Jesus Christ has promised to show up, to walk with us, and to be in us all our days.

Jesus said to Thomas, *"Do you believe because you see me? How happy are those who believe without seeing me!"* It is the call for each of us, to finally let go, to abandon ourselves in the mystery of the presence of the risen Christ. We are strengthened by him in order to affirm with our words and with our life, the same words as Thomas used, *"My Lord and my God."*

"But these have been written in order that you may believe that Jesus is the Messiah, the Son of God, and that through your faith in him you may have life."

Reflection

Summer has arrived, bringing construction to the street in front of my home and roadblocks with arrows pointing in different directions. Roadblocks frustrate us, and often we avoid certain routes because of all the detours we find. Eventually repairs will be finished, the new road will be smoother, and traffic will flow easily. We quickly forget that our way had been slowed down or altered for a time.

In that same way, we all face roadblocks to our faith at different times in our lives. And it is at these times that we are at risk of getting lost. Fear of the unknown and anxiety have been close companion of mine for most of my life. My mother used to tell a story about me when I was about five, and she was trying to get me to go to a Sunday School class. But I was determined not to leave her. She pointed out another younger child who needed some reassurance, and off I went to help out someone younger and needier than myself. When I could help someone else, or work on a cause or organization that I deemed worthwhile, fear vanished.

Recently, my daughter, Rachel, her children, and I were out for a ride in her neighborhood. We passed an older man who was sitting on a sloping lawn next to his lawn mower.

"Wait," said Rachel. "Back up, Mom." When we came to the man and stopped, she got out and went over to talk with him. We discovered he had fallen and could not get up. He was breathing heavily. Rachel kindly suggested that he hire some help with his lawn.

"No," he said. "That would be giving in."

After we helped him up, his wife assisted him to the house. We worried about him as we left.

I could not help but reflect on the fear expressed by this man, the fear of growing old, or of becoming a burden, of needing help for the daily chores. All of us want to be self-sufficient and to be able to do things for ourselves. Meaning in our lives seems to be dependent on our ability to do things, to accomplish things. When that is taken away by old age or disease or an accident, we come face to face with the fear of meaninglessness—surely the heart of doubt.

I have a dear friend, Dan, who has had to come to terms with life in a wheel chair after a devastating bicycle accident. Yet years of pain and the loss of an active lifestyle have not destroyed him. Today he spends several days a week volunteering at a children's home, helping kids with their studies. He is one of my heroes.

I think I was in college when I first doubted that God was in charge of the world, or that there even was a God. Depression hit me hard my third year, when I was taking some tough classes and had become involved in campus leadership activities. It was also a time of social unrest following the assassination of John F. Kennedy, and with the freedom marches raising racial tension. Questions of justice and why bad things happen to good people made me struggle to believe.

Doubt creeps in. It does not often barge in, announcing itself, scoffing at other truths. It is far subtler. Times of doubt for me have often been when failures or perceived wrongs pile up and pull me down. I take everything personally. That person doesn't like me. Over there, they don't think I'm doing a good job. Oh, no, I'm late once again.

Sometimes it is global problems: why are there so many poor children going hungry every night and dying of easily cured diseases every day? Why are there so many wars and so many evil leaders murdering their own people or lying and stealing the people's money? Why do we in this country take our clean land, air, and water for granted, and waste so many of our resources, day in and day out?

Sometimes it is church and church politics. I have often thought about how much fun the devil has disrupting Christian fellowship and learning and worship through jealousy, ego, dishonesty, and laziness. The more Christians of every sort try to assert their own power or influence in the church, the more the church suffers from disagreements, and, therefore, the less the Gospel is truly heard and the sacraments received.

Congregations tend to grow when people hear "feel good" messages along with spirited music, so they can leave church on a high. Not that God wants us to live life in fear and trembling or to feel that to truly worship God we must be sad and serious. But living a life of faith is not all ups and upper ups, either. God calls us to believe and to trust, even when things look bad, when we lose our loved one, are fired from our job, or mess up a relationship.

It is easy to trust God and have faith when things are going our way. It is not easy when darkness swirls around us, when the path is not lit, and when fear takes an icy hold on our soul. But when doubt creeps in we need to pay attention to our devotional life, to what anchors us in good times and bad.

I have a favorite print hanging on the inner wall of my family room, painted by Joe Geshick, an Ojibway artist who grew up in northern Minnesota not far from my hometown of Virginia. The print is large, covering most of the wall, and its images blend with and continue into the leather frame, created by an artist friend of mine at Warrior Works in Hill City, South Dakota. Stark in its simplicity, it is also subtly complex in its composition. The painting depicts a Native American sitting in a canoe, and both he and the canoe are split between light and darkness. The large sun-like circle in the light represents God. Three dots below the figure represent the spirit, while a line connects humans to the spiritual world. The figure in the canoe holds tobacco in his outstretched hand, which was used in spiritual ceremonies. The work is called "The Feeding of the Spirit."

This painting speaks to me of many things. We are often caught between light and darkness in our lives, facing an important decision, or poised to take off or to stagnate. The light represents God's love and forgiveness, while the darkness is the absence of God. The peacefulness of a canoe on still water evokes quiet joy, tranquility, and fulfillment in life's journey. The solitary experience of the canoeist points to the individuality of our relationship with God and of our devotional life. Finally, the canoe and its paddler are headed toward the light—the light of day and of eternal life.

For the canoeist, there are no roadblocks, only the journey embracing both light and dark. On days when I feel stuck and need spiritual centering and energy, I look at that painting and let its power soak into me.

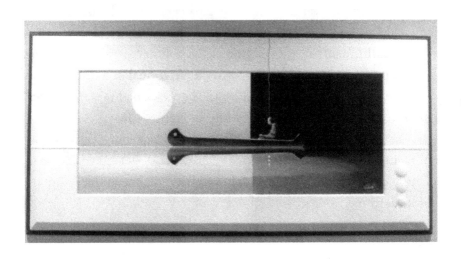

Amazing Grace

21 But now God's way of putting people right with himself has been revealed. It has nothing to do with law, even though the Law of Moses and the prophets gave their witness to it. 22 God puts people right through their faith in Jesus Christ. God does this to all who believe in Christ, because there is no difference at all: 23 everyone has sinned and is far away from God's saving presence. 24 But by the free gift of God's grace all are put right with him through Christ Jesus, who sets them free. 25 God offered him, so that by his blood he should become the means by which people's sins are forgiven through their faith in him. God did this in order to demonstrate that he is righteous. In the past he was patient and overlooked people's sins; but in the present time he deals with their sins, in order to demonstrate his righteousness. In this way God shows that he himself is righteous and that he puts right everyone who believes in Jesus. Romans 3:21-26

Amazing Grace, how sweet the sound...

I stepped into the dying room of the hospital. I'd been there many times before, but the incense of death and fear made me catch my breath. Why was I here? He surely didn't want me. Nurses had told me how he had asked other pastors to leave. But I had promised his wife.

He looked past me with that vacant, thousand yard stare of the combat fatigued. Under the sheet stamped Falls Memorial Hospital, he was as rigid as a four by ten oak plank. He was filled with cancer. He knew it. He was afraid.

In my stumbling way, I mentioned something about my name being Pastor Jerstad and would he like to visit. Silence. I felt uneasy. Why was I here? I didn't know what to do or say. I was sure I was only adding to his misery. Nuts, I thought, I'm getting out of here. "Would you like me to pray with you?" You know, when in doubt, say a prayer. Silence.

"Father, this man, too, is one of your children, whom you love very much. Please be with him now. Amen." Overcome with mixed feelings of grief for that man locked in a prison of fear and death, and at the same time feeling like a jerk as a pastor, I turned to leave.

And then it happened. His hand snaked out and grabbed mine. And he would not let go. His eyes captured mine and then filled with tears. Tears slid down my cheeks and got lost in my beard. If I shifted my weight, he'd squeeze my hand tighter and would not let go. Five minutes went by. Ten. Longer. There we were, a hack preacher and an old logger holding hands, staring at each other, crying. Then he closed his eyes, dropped my hand, and his body became as relaxed as a nursing child. Peace had replaced fear. "See you tomorrow," I said. And I did. I walked into his room, he held out his hand, and we went through the same litany, scripture, prayers, and holding hands and sharing peace and comfort with our eyes and tears. And that is how he died.

Amazing grace. Not your typical conversion experience. But could it be? Could it be that it was God's Holy Spirit who invaded the darkness and the stench of that cancer-filled, hopeless man and filled him with His presence, overcame him with His love, washed him in forgiveness and enshrouded him in peace? Amazing grace!

Let us not put limits on the grace of our Lord Jesus. Let us not cheapen it, take it for granted, neglect or abuse that gift. And let us not turn it into a new law, a series of have-to's: you have to do this, you have to give up that, you have to believe this way, you have to have that kind of experience. No. Grace, the totally undeserved love and favor of our Lord toward each one of us, is a want-to, a gift for all, a gift of love, a gift far more powerful, wide sweeping, merciful, and forgiving than we can begin to fathom.

Listen again to his gracious word for you: *"Everyone has sinned and is far away from God's saving presence. But by the free gift of God's grace all are put right with him through Christ Jesus, who sets them free."* But God's mercy is so abundant, and his love for us is so great, that while we were spiritually dead in our disobedience he brought us to life with Christ.

By God's grace, you have been saved. God did this to demonstrate for all time to come the extraordinary greatness of his grace in the love he showed us in Christ Jesus. It is by God's grace that you have been saved through faith. It is not the result of your own efforts, but God's gift. Amazing grace!

Let everyone know that grace is amazing, sufficient and redemptive. And when we are burned out by the flaming word that coursed through us, when we are consumed at last by that amazing grace blazing through us, and when we, who have been privileged to translate the truth of God's grace, are finally translated from earth to heaven, then bear us away gently, blow a muted trumpet and lay us down softly. Place a two-edged sword on our coffins and raise a tune triumphant, for we were brave soldiers of the Word, and before we died we had become speakers for our God, living in and sharing that amazing grace.

Reflection

My memories of Mark and his influence on my life grow stronger with time. A week ago, I sat with two men who work to help solve the huge problem of addiction to drugs and alcohol. They spoke of their plans and ideas and the future of their program. Finally I said, "You know, there are four people at this table. Mark would have loved this program, because he spent a great deal of time working with Alcoholics Anonymous in International Falls. And because you are dreaming big."

Mark's passion for helping people and for dreaming big dreams were two of his greatest gifts. The years right before he was diagnosed with terminal cancer were filled with great plans for the Good Samaritan Society. The national campus was to be the top teaching-learning center for long-term care in the United States, maybe even the world.

The campus was to be transformed with a large performing arts and worship chapel, a wellness center for seniors, a retreat center, a nursing home, an assisted living center and independent living duplexes. An award-winning architect from Minneapolis was chosen to design the buildings. All this was in the works until the dreaded words "terminal cancer" were spoken.

Mark often told his children to dream big. His attitude certainly wore off on me, but then that was pretty much how I did things anyway, 110% effort or not at all.

I am an activist. Wherever there is injustice, I want to take up that cause. And often do. Sometimes this trait serves me well. Sometimes not so well. When I attended St. Olaf College, women had hours. If you were a freshman, it was 10:30 p.m. every night except Friday and Saturday, when we were allowed to stay out to the very late hour of 11:30 or midnight. Men had no hours.

If you were a woman, you had a strict dress code: dresses or skirts had to be worn every day outside your dorm except Saturday mornings. Believe me, it was bone-chilling in the winter fighting the fury of the frigid wind on Manitou Heights as I crossed campus with bare legs. When the freshmen women were to visit the President's home, corridor by corridor, we had to wear gloves and a hat. Men had no dress code.

Finally, men could smoke on campus, indoors or out of doors, and women could not. So I began a campaign during my senior year to establish a little equality. Even though I did not smoke, I advocated for equal smoking rights for women on campus. And won! Now, of course, I wonder at my choice of causes, but then it seemed important.

The activist part of me always wants to be "doing" something to help whatever it is that needs helping. While I think this is mainly a good quality, I can easily overstep my bounds and cause trouble for myself. This usually happens in discussions with other folks when I get a little too excited about the topic. But there was an incident early in my life that taught me a good lesson.

On a sun-draped summer afternoon when I was about six, I was out in my back yard when my cat, Freckles, proudly trotted up to me with a mouse in her mouth. Poor mouse, I thought, and without any further thinking, I grabbed hold of its tail and freed it from the teeth that wanted to preserve it for some playing before eating it for dinner. The mouse quickly followed mouse instincts and sunk its incisors into my thumb. The result, of course, was immediate freedom for the mouse, and immediate and deep pain for me. Just trying to help out.

Part of me always wants to make sense out of things and then do something about it. When I took a course on Kierkegaard with Dr. Howard Hong, he helped me think about life in a different way in regard to being and doing. He tried to make me understand that it was important to just "be," and sometimes that was enough.

And that is the connection to this sermon. Mark wanted to preach the Gospel in every sermon. Luther would have nodded his approval. It is not about what we do in our lives that gives us salvation, but God's grace in Christ through his word.

And yet we live with the paradox—grace comes as undeserved and unearned and still we are volitional creatures who make choices and who are told to love and care for the poor and needy and bear one another's burdens.

Recently I received a poignant email from my Godson, Danny Wilcox. "I'll be graduating with a degree in Philosophy and creative writing and I want to put my skills to use working for social change. There are so many things I see in the world that could be better that I'm not sure where to start or what work would be most fulfilling and productive for my personality…. I want to make the world a better place, I'm just not sure how to do that," he writes.

How to do that? Danny realizes he is reflective where others are more action-oriented, and he wonders how to incorporate this skill into his life's work. Again the dichotomy—being and doing.

God loved Mark both when he did something—went to the patient's room and prayed, and when he just sat with him. God loved the man both when he lay there in anguish doing nothing and when he reached out his hand.

Being and doing. We love God's people through activism of one kind or another, as a response to God's grace, but always knowing we can never do a thing to earn our way into God's good graces.

He Is Alive!

13 On that same day two of Jesus' followers were going to a village named Emmaus, about seven miles from Jerusalem, 14 and they were talking to each other about all the things that had happened. 15 As they talked and discussed, Jesus himself drew near and walked along with them; 16 they saw him, but somehow did not recognize him. 17 Jesus said to them, "What are you talking about to each other, as you walk along?" They stood still, with sad faces. 18 One of them, named Cleopas, asked him, "Are you the only visitor in Jerusalem who doesn't know the things that have been happening there these last few days?" 19 "What things?" he asked. "The things that happened to Jesus of Nazareth," they answered. "This man was a prophet and was considered by God and by all the people to be powerful in everything he said and did. 20 Our chief priests and rulers handed him over to be sentenced to death, and he was crucified. 21 And we had hoped that he would be the one who was going to set Israel free! Besides all that, this is now the third day since it happened. 22 Some of the women of our group surprised us; they went at dawn to the tomb, 23 but could not find his body. They came back saying they had seen a vision of angels who told them that he is alive. 24 Some of our group went to the tomb and found it exactly as the women had said, but they did not see him." 25 Then Jesus said to them, "How foolish you are, how slow you are to believe everything the prophets said! 26 Was it not necessary for the Messiah to suffer these things and then to enter his glory?" 27 And Jesus explained to them what was said about himself in all the Scriptures, beginning with the books of Moses and the writings of all the prophets. 28 As they came near the village to which they were going, Jesus acted as if he were going farther; 29 but they held him back, saying, "Stay with us; the day is almost over and it is getting dark." So he went in to stay with them. 30 He sat down to eat with them, took the bread, and said the blessing; then he broke the bread and gave it to them. 31 Then their eyes were opened and they recognized him, but he disappeared from their sight. Luke 24:13-31

When a wonderful and majestic life suddenly comes to a tragic end, there is no way that we can call that death good news. Dietrich Bonhoeffer, Lutheran pastor, theologian and author, was part of the resistance against Hitler, saving countless Jews from persecution and death. He was executed by the SS Black Guard just days before the Allies would have rescued him. No way can we call his death good news. And if all we could say was that God became incarnate, became flesh among us, and in love died for us all, and that was the end—crucified, dead and buried—there is no way in the world we could call that good news. It would simply be another example of the old case we know oh so well—that death is, in fact, the final victor.

In the writings of the New Testament, the first followers of Jesus did not expect him to die at the hands of the Romans. And when he did, they did not expect him to be raised again. They suffered from a double reversal as it were. God, in Jesus Christ, died and then they thought that was the end of it. Then he rose again. And in the midst of all of that, there was rampant confusion, confusion that lasts to this day. But one thing is clear. And it is this: that things were not as they seemed to be. There was a reversal. Things were twisted. Death had been defeated. Resurrection was rampant. Victory was won through Jesus Christ. And that reversal has a multitude of implications. One of them is this: it is simply that life is not as you expect it to be. Life is different in this world. If you see that, to the extent that you believe in the resurrection, and can see little pictures of the resurrection happening again and again in your life, you experience that resurrection paradigm.

I experienced it again last night. I crawled into bed, and, as I always do, I prayed for people who had touched my life that day. I remembered our long trip from northern Minnesota, where we visited my wife's mother, and I remembered dropping my wife off in Minneapolis to coach her softball team, as they played the University of Minnesota. I thought about my feelings as I lay in bed. Poor Sandy. Who does she think she is, anyway? A university of 50,000 students against little Augustana College with 1500 students. Crazy lady, crazy idea. Why?! God bless her. I fell asleep.

Deep into my REM sleep, from deep in my subconscious, suddenly, I felt myself being attacked. What was going on?! And then, I heard the words. At first I didn't understand. Someone was shaking me and screaming right in my ear: "We won!!!"

And there it was—a little paradigm. The resurrection happening again. The unexpected. The reversal. That which seemed impossible was possible.

This is a little picture of how Christians experience resurrection in the world. Things are not as they seem. There is hope indeed.

Easter is two women going to the tomb preparing a body for burial, hands laden with spices, finding the stone rolled away and the tomb empty.

Easter is two men walking along the road to Emmaus, saddened, and then being met by a third, and sharing with that person the tragedy of their life, how they fell apart when the one they had trusted and hoped in had been killed.

Easter is inviting that person to have a meal with them at the end of the day, and then, in the breaking of the bread, recognizing that person as the Lord himself.

Easter is running to Jerusalem to tell the others what had happened, that they had seen the Lord.

Easter is hope. Newness. Reversal of what seems to be. Easter is gift and celebration indeed.

As we contemplate Easter, and think about it for us, we know this much: At the very least Easter means that in our God-given freedom, no matter how much we seek to wreck and destroy each other and the world, there is no way we can take the compassion of God, nail it to a cross, put it in a tomb, and come back three days later and expect it to still be there. He is risen! With that there is hope.

What does that mean? Well, for one thing, it means that we who are believers, who hang on and are hung onto by that Easter faith, that resurrection faith, can celebrate. This is Good News! We, as Christians, need to remember Easter on a daily basis, rather than wallow in doubt and fear. We can have joy in our hearts. He is risen! Death is defeated! That is the promise for each of us. What a gift! Celebrate! He is alive!

Easter can be compared to a child who gets lost in a large city as night falls and the rain pours down. The child huddles under a bridge, frightened to death, expecting the worst. Frigid, fearful hours pass. But then in the distance, a pinpoint of light, a figure walking. The child sees his father, and relief and joy flood over him. His father takes his big old raincoat and wraps it around the child and holds him close. He brings him home. Mother and father together fix a meal, and he eats. As he starts to warm up, he tells of his experiences—what it is like to be out there in that world, cold and frightened. How he was almost hit by a car, how he could not find any place to get warm, and how people never listened to him. And then what it was like to be found by his father.

Easter is like that. But there is more. Easter is also an invitation, a knock on the door. For some of us who have been touched by the Gospel, our vision is still limited. We sense that the whole purpose of what we are is simply to be found. We rest safely and securely, snuggled up in the warmth of the church, as if that is enough. We miss the whole point that there is always a knock on the door, an invitation to come out into the world, having been warmed by the fires of the resurrection, to come out and follow our Lord's leading.

Of course, when we follow, we must realize where we will be led. Know this: you will be led past mountains of ammunition, piles of bombs. You will be led into hospitals, into nursing homes where old people are silent or babble away in memory of better times. You will be led into the fray of life, and your heart will be broken. And only the most naïve will not realize that you are being led once again to the crucifixion.

Perhaps then it is safest to stay inside where it is warm. Unless, you have gone to the tomb and seen that it is empty and have been captured by that resurrection hope and faith, and are drawn out to spend your life for the sake of others, never counting the cost, living by the strength and the hope of that resurrection faith. He is alive!

Reflection

Luke's story about the men on the way to Emmaus, one of my favorites, is filled with images—friends walking on a dusty road, talking, listening and learning, and then their begging Jesus to stay with them. The revelation that takes place produces unbelievable joy. From complete despair to exploding joy! The Mormon Tabernacle Choir sings a poignantly beautiful song on that theme: Stay with us; the day is nearly over.

We have just begun the season of Lent, as I reflect on Mark's sermon. Appropriately, winter still has us in its icy grip, and where some melting has occurred, everything is dirty brown. The sky is leaden with a bluish hue, the day shutting down, as the words "reversal," "invitation," and "safety" sink into my soul.

Reversal. Invitation. Safety. These are BIG words for me.

Reversal. When I think of reversal, I think of a change for the better. I know it can go the other way, but I prefer to focus on the positive aspect. Mark's example of my softball team from little Augustana taking on the University of Minnesota on their home field—and winning—on a night when we had more fans in the stands than they did, and they all had snowmobile suits or were tucked into sleeping bags, or both, was perfect. As a coach and as a player, you have to keep hope alive, hope for a reversal of fortune. In every game. Hope against hope.

I will never forget the day we played in the North Central Conference Championship hosted by the University of Nebraska, Omaha, on one of those nasty spring days with off and on rain, heavy clouds, a north wind and the temperature hanging in the upper 40s. We had played Mankato State in the double-elimination semi-final round and lost. Their team went to the warmth and nourishment of the restaurant while our team warmed up to play our arch-rivals and host team, UNO. We won in a tightly contested 1-0 game.

Rested, warmed up and fed, Mankato was back, confident of a win. After all, they had two pitchers, both rested, and we were down to one, Amy Jorgenson, who had already pitched one game. Fortunately we won the flip and were the home team. Playing for the NCC championship, the first game went back and forth. Finally, in the 12th inning, we scored and won.

The final game was also very close. We scored a run in the 10th inning and won the NCC Championship! A huge reversal of fortune.

Invitation. When I was about four, I used to creep downstairs from my bedroom and from the bottom step, look around the corner at my mom, dad, and brother eating breakfast at the kitchen table. I continued looking, just my head visible, until my mom or dad saw me and invited me to come to the table. Being invited, being included has always been a big thing for me. And conversely, not being included has been my Achilles' heel. Perhaps part of this response is due to abandonment by my birth mother, and part is due to my inherent shyness.

When we first moved to Sioux Falls, I met Linda Pashby while working at the State Penitentiary High School. We became friends, and she, in turn, introduced me to her bridge club, a small group of women who had known each other since college. I did not know how to play bridge (that was not big at St. Olaf), but soon the group stopped playing bridge in lieu of intriguing and hilarious conversations. We met monthly in homes, and that invitation meant the world to me. We are still friends to this day.

Safety. I do not know quite when it started, probably in high school. My anxiety level, especially during certain events, almost paralyzed me. I disliked being in front of people, even in a group. I spent much of my free time at home instead of out socializing. I poured myself into my studies. In high school!

I hoped for change when I went to college, and I loved my freshman year. But not long after my sophomore year began, my mood plummeted, and I struggled to shake off the gloomy feeling. Fortunately, I started dating Mark, and life turned around. An invitation led to a reversal and brought about safety!

These days life has a lovely rhythm, and I have time to visit with friends and to pay attention to the small parts of my life. Serenity surrounds my days and gives me joy. I have been loved and included and now reach out to others, and I no longer am afraid. I can only say the peace of God that passes all understanding wraps around me like a robe every day, and I am grateful. Through the many small crucifixions and resurrections I have experienced, I have come to trust the power of God to restore me, no matter what happens.

Sandy and Mark, a St. Olaf Romance

The Lost Sheep

1 One day when many tax collectors and other outcasts came to listen to Jesus, 2 the Pharisees and the teachers of the Law started grumbling, "This man welcomes outcasts and even eats with them!" 3 So Jesus told them this parable: 4 "Suppose one of you has a hundred sheep and loses one of them—what do you do? You leave the other ninety-nine sheep in the pasture and go looking for the one that got lost until you find it. 5 When you find it, you are so happy that you put it on your shoulders 6 and carry it back home. Then you call your friends and neighbors together and say to them, 'I am so happy I found my lost sheep. Let us celebrate!' 7 In the same way, I tell you, there will be more joy in heaven over one sinner who repents than over ninety-nine respectable people who do not need to repent.

8 "Or suppose a woman who has ten silver coins loses one of them—what does she do? She lights a lamp, sweeps her house, and looks carefully everywhere until she finds it. 9 When she finds it, she calls her friends and neighbors together, and says to them, 'I am so happy I found the coin I lost. Let us celebrate!' 10 In the same way, I tell you, the angels of God rejoice over one sinner who repents."

11 Jesus went on to say, "There was once a man who had two sons. 12 The younger one said to him, 'Father, give me my share of the property now.' So the man divided his property between his two sons. 13 After a few days the younger son sold his part of the property and left home with the money. He went to a country far away, where he wasted his money

in reckless living. 14 He spent everything he had. Then a severe famine spread over that country, and he was left without a thing. 15 So he went to work for one of the citizens of that country, who sent him out to his farm to take care of the pigs. 16 He wished he could fill himself with the bean pods the pigs ate, but no one gave him anything to eat. 17 At last he came to his senses and said, 'All my father's hired workers have more than they can eat, and here I am about to starve! 18 I will get up and go to my father and say, "Father, I have sinned against God and against you. 19 I am no longer fit to be called your son; treat me as one of your hired workers."' 20 So he got up and started back to his father. He was still a long way from home when his father saw him; his heart was filled with pity, and he ran, threw his arms around his son, and kissed him."
Luke 15: 1-20

One of the fond memories I have of my growing-up years is that, periodically, our family would spend time in the Colorado Rockies, near Mt. Meeker. That place has especially fond memories for me because Sandy and I spent our honeymoon there. A beautiful place. I have many memories from that lovely spot, but the one that stands out in a particularly poignant way happened a number of years ago when my brother was much younger than he is now, and we had decided to spend the day climbing Mt. Meeker. Some of us climbed to the top and others walked shorter distances, so we were not all in a big herd. We went in different directions, and on the way down, my little brother got separated from the rest of the family. One group thought he was with another group, and another group was sure he was with the other group. Everybody was sure he was taken care of. But he wasn't.

When we came back, counted faces, and realized John was not there, we started looking around—first the cabin, and then taking short hikes. Evening came. Still no John. Finally, Dad said, "We're going to have to go back up the mountain." Then he looked at me and the rest of us—I will never forget the look in his eyes and across his face, all composure gone and only raw, gut, honest feelings there. He looked at me and said, "Mark, I want my boy back!" Well, we found him. Everything was fine.

Our Gospel text for today has that same kind of urgency ringing through it. Jesus tells two simple little stories, but in the midst of those stories runs that urgency, that desperation, of a loving parent for a lost child—"I want my boy back; I want my girl back!"—that tells us something fundamental about God, something at the core of his very being as he has revealed himself to us. And that is this: Our God, our Lord, is a seeker, and he is after us, each one of us, relentlessly in a multiplicity of ways. And he will never give up. He wants us! God is a seeker.

Our text tells us a number of things. I'd like to highlight quickly three considerations for us about our seeking God. Number one—he is persistent, relentless, and tenacious as a bulldog. He never gives up, never, ever. He is after you. I don't want you to get paranoid, but I am going to tell you a secret and tell you the truth right now. He is after you every day of your life, every breathing moment that you have. Know this, no matter what you are, no matter where you are, no matter what you're engaged in, he is after you and will never give up.

That search started a long time ago. You know the biblical account, centering in the cross and the resurrection of Jesus and continuing down through time and through space to the time when you were brought before the congregation. Most of you were held in your parents' arms, perhaps screaming, and the pastor said in his very best pastor's voice, "I baptize you in the name of the Father and the Son and the Holy Spirit."

More than water and word, this is sacrament, God present, reaching out, claiming you for his very own. God is tenacious. That tenacity continued in the little Sunday School room where you learned that "Jesus loves me" and in those confirmation classes that many of you took, where you were more concerned about the girl or guy sitting next to you than what was being taught, and yet somehow something filtered through. He continues to this point, seeking after you, wanting you. Every time you hear a word proclaimed about the love of God, that word is more than just a message or a sermon. God is after you, trying to touch you, letting you know he is there, and that he wants you. God is tenacious. God will never give up. His very nature is to keep seeking, no matter what you do, no matter who you are. There is no sin so dark that it excludes him; no doubt so hopeless that he is not there at the very core and bottom of it. God is after you. God loves you. God wants you.

Secondly, this text tells us a little something about the nature of the God who seeks you. When he found the sheep, what did the shepherd do? Put it up on his shoulders and carried it home rejoicing. He did not grab it by the ear, drag it along, saying, "You dirty, rotten sheep! What are you doing, getting away from here? I'm going to teach you a lesson you'll never forget!" No! That's parents! That's me! That's not God. He cradles the sheep around his shoulders, holding it gently.

There is a loving, gentle, caring touch to God's seeking of you. Do not forget it. Know, when you are in your deepest pain, that, ultimately, pain is there for a reason and the reason is the love underneath. It hurts to go through surgery to carve out a cancer, but that very surgery is what can save your life.

Know that God deals with you, with each one of you, and with us as a congregation and as a community, lovingly, caringly, gently. That is God's nature. And, when that sheep was found or the coin was found, what happened? Did the old lady who found her coin say, "Boy, I'm glad I've got this thing? I'm not going to tell anybody because then they'd know what a jerk I was for losing it in the first place!"

No, she called the friends and the neighbors together, and said, "Let's have a party! That which was lost is found!" And the feeling that flows right through this text is the theme of joy, of celebration, of a party. There is more joy in heaven over one sinner who repents. Think of it! Think of the laughter, the good times. God says, "Great news! Got another one in!" Joy! Phenomenal!

Picturesque language, to be sure. But language is all we have to help us understand. And this language describes the very nature of God, who is after you and who loves you and treats you tenderly. As he gathers you back again, joy and celebration abounds. A powerful text! But you remember the context. Lest you wonder if this text is for you, let's go back and think for a moment. Jesus is sitting around with the castoffs of the community.

There is a prostitute over there, and the guy who's got the problem drinking over there. There is a bunch of unemployed and some of the sick and the gross. And Jesus is very much at home talking, bantering back and forth. Surrounding them stand some of the Pharisees, the self-righteous ones, who say, "Look at the guy! He's gathering with sinners and outcasts, and he's even eating with them!" That is why Jesus told the story. Some of us may feel like outcasts. We have a load of guilt and brokenness, a secret to all but ourselves that makes us feel totally, absolutely unaccepted, and we wonder why we even go to worship. Know this. Jesus is after you, to offer you love and forgiveness, to pour his grace richly upon you, to make you his own.

Some of us may have an inflated opinion of ourselves and of our religiosity and of our holiness, and we go to worship because we always go. This story is for you as well, to know that the Lord sees through that, and if you get broken down it is all right because he is using it to build you up, to heal you in a new way, to surround you with his love, to make you his own. The story is for all of us. How does this work in life? I conclude by sharing a little story with you.

Last week, I was sitting in a friend's living room with two

other friends. We were reminiscing about the recent death of their eight-year-old daughter to leukemia. Her mom talked about how, there in the hospital, she will never forget, as long as she lives on this earth, those little, frail hands of her daughter grabbing onto her and crying, "Mom, Mom, Mom!" just moments before she died. And we talked about the diary she had found after she died, and about some of the things that were in it. Things like, "Dear Diary, today I had a fight with Mom and Dad. I won. Love, Kim"

We were talking about little notes and letters that people had sent from all over. Then she said, "Oh, you've got to see these!" She went over and pulled out a packet. Here were notes from little Kim's fourth-grade class. Two stood out. They were buried in the middle of the pile, one right above the other. One said, "Kim was my best friend. I really loved her. My heart is broken." The next one had a sticker on it, the kind little kids love to paste on their letters. The note said this, "Dear Mr. and Mrs. Walter, hang in there! Love, John." She looked up at me and said, "Can you believe it? Hang in there! Hang in there. That's what we're trying to do. And the Lord will help us."

Each of us is lost, I suppose, one way or another every day—lost in all that we seem to have to do, lost in the guilt that we may struggle with, lost in the question mark that is our future. We are lost in the absence of friends, lost in the quality of our relationships, lost in the struggle we're trying to go through in terms of our emerging moral and ethical values, lost in the journey as far as our faith is concerned. We all know what it is like to be lost in one way or another. Know this: our Lord is a seeker, and he is after you. He will find you. He loves you, and he wants you to be his forever.

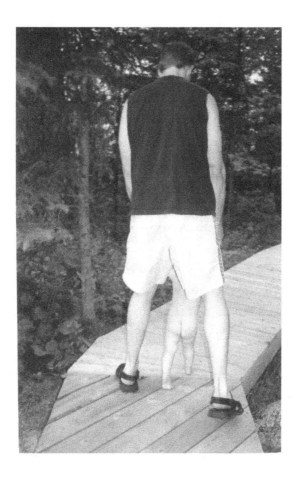

Reflection

I like the spin Mark puts on these two exemplary parables Jesus told to his disciples. I used to think that whatever a preacher said from the pulpit was true. I grew out of that sometime in adolescence, earlier than I grew out of believing in a literal translation of the Bible. But I think Mark was really onto something with this particular interpretation. And since he had studied both Greek and advanced Hebrew, he did have a leg up on interpretation.

Could God ever love a sinner so much that God would have

a big party when that person returned?! There are some pretty dark folks out there, who do some awful things and definitely do not have love in their hearts. And then there is me. I commit sins of commission and omission every day. And yet God still seeks us all out.

Alas, God's tenacity and my tenacity are two different things. This sermon reminds me of a time in my life I wish had never happened, but it did. I was with my softball team, and Mike, 6, and Sarah, 4, were with me, too. In the school van, we drove across town to a field where we were scheduled to play another team. As a coach, I always focused on my team and the game, even though in those early days the city field we played on was poor and our equipment and uniforms were minimal at best. Mike and Sarah ran off to play on the swing set. It was a warm spring day, with the sun high in the afternoon sky. After the game was over, we loaded up our team in the two vans and drove back to the college, where we unloaded the equipment, put it away, and had a team meeting.

Then one of my players asked me, "Where are Mike and Sarah?" WHERE ARE MIKE AND SARAH?!!! My heart stopped. My legs starting racing toward the van before my mind could take in the reality of what I had done, or actually, had not done. I HAD FORGOTTEN MY CHILDREN AT THE PARK!!!!

It took me a good ten minutes to get to the park, and during that time I died a thousand deaths, raging at my stupidity and my lack of focus on my children, tormented by horrible thoughts about where Mike and Sarah might be and how frightened they must be.

As in the story Jesus told, this story had a happy ending. Shortly after I drove off, Sarah looked around for me. I was nowhere to be seen and she started crying. Mike told her not to cry, and then he started crying. Before long a young couple came over and asked what the matter was. Finding out they had been left in the park (abandoned by an irresponsible parent, I assume they thought), they were able to find out the address from Mike and take them home. Mike and Sarah have never let me forget that incident, and if they continue teasing me until I die, I will deserve it.

Human parents fail in many ways, but the tenacity of God, as portrayed in this sermon, never fails. I am reminded of many things. One of them is a story my mother told me. When she was growing up on a farm outside Mitchell, South Dakota, in the early 1900s it was a tough time for family farms, and hers was no exception. One had to be really tenacious to stay. There was drought, brutal winter blizzards, and dust storms, not to mention grasshoppers that ate everything except people. My mother's personal life was hard also. Her mother had fallen during her second pregnancy and could not have any more children, so my mother had no one to play with on that farm. Her mom was a tough-love person, something of a "tiger mom."

My mom threatened to run away from home more than once and finally carried out her threat when she was about eight. When her mother realized that Phoebe had actually left the farm, she crawled up onto the highest building—probably the hog barn—and looked up and down the dirt roads. She could barely make out a cloud of dust, where the sheep dog was running in circles around her daughter, doing what good sheep dogs do, trying to herd the runaway home. The lost was found.

A more recent story of lost and found began at appropriately named Lost Bay. Shortly after Mark and I bought our cabin, we decided to take a quick boat ride one afternoon to look around and to find a site for the sauna we planned to build the following summer. It was late October, with a deep chill in the air. After an hour or so, I observed a snowflake or two come down, and I told Mark, "We need to go." We headed down to the end of our bay westward toward our boat dock.

In front of us was a curtain of white, thick snow, which, combined with the late gray afternoon, made us wonder if we were going in the right direction. Were we lost? We almost hit a deer swimming to an island, driving our fear deeper. We kept on going. Finally, we saw the lights of the resort and landed, filled with joy to be safely back, at a dock covered with thick snow.

In my life, feeling lost was not always physical. At times I felt depressed following the death of my father, who was my best friend. The fact that our family was radically changed with his absence also gave me the feeling that my life was turned upside down.

As an adult, I was given the opportunity to coach women's sports at a Division II college for 27 years, which was a gift in my life. But learning on the job was not easy, and I often felt lost. I took my cues from my student-athletes, from other coaches, and from games and clinics. Finally in the last several years I felt as if I knew what I was doing.

Looking back on a full life, I am grateful. Even in the worst times, I always felt God loved me and would care for me. And though I was, at times, lost, I never felt abandoned. This gift of faith gives me hope and peace, knowing that at the end of our lives God will bring us safely home.

On the Other Hand

Immediately following the transfiguration text in Luke, we find this little story:

28 About a week after he had said these things, Jesus took Peter, John, and James with him and went up a hill to pray. 29 While he was praying, his face changed its appearance, and his clothes became dazzling white. 30 Suddenly two men were there talking with him. They were Moses and Elijah, 31 who appeared in heavenly glory and talked with Jesus about the way in which he would soon fulfill God's purpose by dying in Jerusalem. 32 Peter and his companions were sound asleep, but they woke up and saw Jesus' glory and the two men who were standing with him. 33 As the men were leaving Jesus, Peter said to him, "Master, how good it is that we are here! We will make three tents, one for you, one for Moses, and one for Elijah." (He did not really know what he was saying.) 34 While he was still speaking, a cloud appeared and covered them with its shadow; and the disciples were afraid as the cloud came over them. 35 A voice said from the cloud, "This is my Son, whom I have chosen—listen to him!" 36 When the voice stopped, there was Jesus all alone. The disciples kept quiet about all this and told no one at that time anything they had seen. Luke 9:28-36

One afternoon, I had a funeral that was one of the most delightful experiences I can ever remember having at a funeral. What a contrast: a funeral and a celebration at the same time. The funeral was for an 86-year-old woman, the mother of a friend. She had died on a Friday morning and was buried Saturday afternoon in a cemetery in Canton, South Dakota, on that beautiful hill that overlooks the town and the prairie. She was buried in a pine box with gorgeous knots in it. The family and a few friends gathered at the little chapel in Our Savior's Lutheran for a memorial service.

Not just a memorial service, this service was filled with contrasts. Before it started, one of her sons stood up and said, "We're glad that you're here. And before we go on with the official part of the funeral, we'd like to have a little family prelude." And this is what it was:

First of all, there was some recorded music from the monastery at Taizé. Beautiful! "Mother liked to pray," he said. "This was some of her favorite music to listen to as she prayed. She listened to this music shortly before she died."

Then he said, "Three of her great-grandchildren were supposed to give a recital today in Minneapolis—a citywide event. They decided to come here instead. So they're going to give their recital here now, in memory of their grandmother."

First he called on a girl, and she was to play a violin. The piece was something I could tell, simply from the title, was going to be heavy duty. I heard the music, but the violinist was hidden from view—I was sitting in the back—until I craned my neck. And here was this little, teeny, sawed-off girl who could not have been more than five. She was playing the violin as if she was 25! It was stunning. An 11-year-old boy was next and played the piano as if he were 21. Last, the 16-year-old brother played a trumpet tune that absolutely knocked the ears right off the sides of our heads. What a contrast. Death, and yet celebration. Life. Recitals. It didn't seem to fit.

The son stood up again, and I thought, Well, now we will get on with the funeral. But I should have known better by then. He said, "We'd like to have a little time of sharing now. So any of you who would like to have a few words about Mother or share any experiences you remember, we invite you now to share."

One stood up, and then another—tears, laughter, little vignettes of her life; grand, overall summations of a life well-lived; and then, finally, he thanked everyone for coming, thanked God for his mother, and turned the service over to the pastor. What a contrast. It didn't seem to fit. And yet, somehow, when it was all wrapped up, nothing could have fit better. It was the best funeral I've ever been to in my life. I'd like to have one like that, but I'm afraid of what would be said, so I'd have them cut out that part, I think.

This Gospel text is another study in contrast: things that do not seem to fit. On first viewing they do not belong. On the one hand, this is the Transfiguration of our Lord, and we have this picture painted for us by the writer of the Gospel of Luke, a picture of Jesus taking three of his disciples, Peter, James, and John, up on top of a hill to pray.

And there, as he is praying, he is transformed, we are told, transfigured in his countenance. He glows. And then figures appear with him—Moses and Elijah. They visit and talk about Jesus' dying, about the way in which he would soon fulfill God's promise. The weary disciples, who seemed to fall asleep whenever Jesus went off to pray, true to form, did so again. But when they awaken, they see this image, this vision, this appearance in front of them. They're overwhelmed. Stunned. They say, "How good it is to be here. Let's build some booths for all of us, so we can just kind of keep this going." Then a cloud comes over, and they are filled with fear. A voice says, "This is my Son. Listen to him." The cloud passes by, and all that's left is Jesus. The disciples, filled with fear, say nothing.

Can you catch the contrasts? On the one hand…, but, on the other hand…. On the one hand, you see light and glory. On the other hand, you've got these disciples sawing wood, sound asleep. On the one hand, we have Jesus talking with Moses and Elijah, the law and the prophets. On the other hand, what are they talking about? About his suffering and his death.

On the one hand, you have the disciples wanting to capture this high, this emotional experience, to savor it, to keep it forever. "Let's just stay here and keep this thing going." On the other hand, the cloud comes over. They are filled with fear. On the one hand, they're on a mountaintop having a rich religious experience. On the other hand, they go down into the valley and there have to do battle with the forces of evil and brokenness and struggle.

What a study in contrast. Nothing seems to fit. Yet, I would be hard-pressed to find a picture that is more pointed as far as our life of faith is concerned. It is a good picture for us, a picture of the contrasts in which we live and walk. On the one hand, we hope for, and many of us have had, rich spiritual experiences that have turned our lives around. I have had those myself, and I treasure them. They have been gifts. But on the other hand, life is not made up of those kinds of highs. Much more happens. We know that contrast all too well.

On the one hand, we know that sense of intimacy, of closeness, those moments when we feel one with the Lord. We feel good about ourselves, freed and forgiven and accepting of ourselves. We feel good about our friends and our neighbors and where we are in our life, we have meaning and purpose in our life, and, for a moment, we have a vision in which all things are clear.

But on the other hand, so much of our life is muddled, and that vision, that experience, dims. We wonder if it was real or if it was simply a figment of our imagination. We're caught up and swept along in a life that pulls us, tugs us and moves us, and we find ourselves constantly behind. We procrastinate. We struggle. We are self-centered in our relationships and less than honest with ourselves and with others. We look to satisfy our own needs rather than reaching out to someone near us who is in need. On the one hand..., on the other hand....

Our life as Christians is filled with this contrast and this struggle. We know only too well, to paraphrase Luther when he talked about sin and grace: At the same time that I'm justified, I'm still struggling as a sinner. What a contrast. This text shows us something that is most profound. I conclude by asking you to simply focus on this in your thoughts and in your life. The mountaintop experiences, when they are given, are given to us not for themselves, not so we can feel good, as wonderful as it is. Rather, Jesus led his disciples back down in the valley and there he went nose to nose with the forces of evil.

If he had not come down, the life of that epileptic, demon-possessed son and the father who was so concerned about his son ("My son, my only son," he said) would never have been changed. It was only in Jesus' coming down and entering into the suffering that this change took place. He invites us, as his disciples, empowered by those special moments—moments of worship, moments of nurturance, moments of receiving his body and blood for forgiveness and for strength—to follow him and move down into the valley, into the life of day-to-day existence where there is suffering and where there is struggle and where our hope sometimes gets tarnished. He urges us to bring his power, his love, his care into our regular, normal, day-to-day life. Empowered by him, we are to be agents of change, to be lovers, to bring healing, to bring hope, to bring community where there is loneliness. It is for you to bring your own little touch of living, loving, forgiving change into the life around you. This is the reason for you to be. This brings the richness to your life. We discover, in the midst of this, the most profound truth.

I spent several months with a woman who was dying slowly of cancer, just being eaten up day by day by day. In the eyes of the world, she became grotesque and then simply disgusting. Her hair fell out, her teeth were suddenly too big for her mouth, her face and her body became jaundiced and had that yellow-golden color. Her eyes were sunken and dark in her head. Her hands suddenly seemed too large for her frail, little arms. She looked as though she had just been transported in time and space from Dachau or Bergenbelsen or Buchenwald.

I would try to visit her two or three times a week, and we would pray or talk, or we would just share silence and hold hands. She would always say, "Thank you," when I left. She said it in Norwegian, *"Takk for alt."* I was with her the day she died, and after we shared some prayers, she asked me to say her favorite Bible verse again. I did and she said, "May I hear it again?" And then it was time beyond words. We shared silence together. That hand, ugly, but beautiful, gave me a little squeeze. She looked at me clearly and said, *"Takk for alt,"* and died. What a contrast. There, in the midst of the suffering and hurt and death, Christ was present, taking her home. There I experienced in the midst of her dying, one of the finest mountaintop experiences of my life.

The truth is this: Jesus meets us, not only on the mountain, but most profoundly in the valley, in our own valleys and in the lives of those who are suffering and who are reaching out to be loved by him through us

Reflection

This sermon resonates with me, both in the way it drops me into my inner darkness and in the ways it makes me explode with laughter. During the last four years, I served in the South Dakota State Senate. Over all, it was an experience rich with new relationships and laced with learning about my state, about government, about politics, and about myself. But I relate to Jesus' exasperation with the people around him: *"How unbelieving and wrong you people are. How long must I stay with you? How long must I put up with you?!"*

If you were a member of the minority party, and I was, respect did not come easily. For one thing, the other party never thought you should get a bill passed, even if it was for the good of the people. (Of course, I thought all of my proposed bills were for the good of the people.)

One of my bills proposed that our state move from a secondary seat belt law (where you are required to buckle up, but law enforcement cannot stop you for that alone) to a primary seat belt law, (where law enforcement officers could ticket you if they saw you were not wearing your seat belt) for which the federal government would give us $5.2 million. More importantly, it would save a minimum of 8 lives per year and prevent 122 traumatic injuries from happening, because the compliance was projected to go from 72% to 83%. Many lives and many dollars, which all of us pay for the cost of medical treatment, are the expensive, painful toll. But my bill, which passed through the Senate Transportation Committee and the Senate floor easily, was halted in the House by another legislator who wanted to take credit for the bill. He killed my bill without being able to get support for a reconsideration—that year or the next. Politics—love it and hate it! On the one hand..., on the other hand....

In a Peanuts' cartoon, Charlie Brown is trying to have Lucy understand that there are ups and downs in life, to which Lucy replies, "I don't want ups and downs! I want all ups and upper ups!" It is, what I suspect, many of us would like. We rationalize about all the dire things that happen in life to us or to others: hardship makes us stronger; there is a silver lining in every cloud; hang in there, everything will be OK in the end.

My mother had a few sayings that covered the situation if you were having a bad day, "If everyone hung up their troubles on the clothesline (we used to have these) in the back yard, everyone would break their necks trying to get their own back again." If I was particularly upset by someone in my life, she would say, "Consider the source." When I would confront her about not listening to me, and always criticizing me for everything I did growing up, while praising nothing, her usual response was, "Well, look how you turned out. Guess I wasn't so bad!"

My father, whom I idolized, died suddenly of a heart attack on November 10, 1957. He was just 53, and I was only 12. He had dropped me off to get my hair cut and then headed to Minneapolis for a school trip for superintendents. That was Wednesday. Saturday evening, when I came home from the movie, my brother told me our father was home but in the hospital with a heart problem. He said he was sure they could fix him.

I sat alone all night in a little rocking chair in front of the window, looking across Silver Lake to the hospital, shaking with fear and loneliness. In the morning, Gladys, my mother's friend, came and got my brother and me and took us to the hospital. We never even got to his room before my mother came down the hall, wailing with grief.

It took me years and years to realize the upside to this painful death. Even though I only had twelve years with my father, I knew beyond a shadow of a doubt that my father loved me, and I experienced a man who loved all the teachers he supervised, who loved and provided for his family, and who instilled in me a love for God and a love for learning. He often put me to bed at night and taught me the Lord's Prayer in Norwegian.

My Father was the only man on our block who would take the neighborhood kids tobogganing at the Eveleth golf course in the winter and stop at Bridgeman's for ice cream on the way home. He never failed to stop and offer a ride to anyone out walking in the winter. He took me hunting and taught me how to fish when I was four. And, at night my father held me in his lap and read stories, or we just listened to the St. Olaf Choir or other classical music from his record collection.

I was four when he took me with him to the St. Olaf campus for his 20th class reunion. Right then and there, I decided I would go to St. Olaf, and I never changed my mind or looked at another school. The direction of my life was changed forever. On the one hand, a father I had dearly loved was taken from me when I was only 12. On the other hand, I eventually realized what a great gift he had been and still was in my life.

A month after my father died, a Christmas concert, featuring the combined high school and junior college choirs and a string ensemble, of which I was a part, was to be held at my junior high school in the huge auditorium, which would be packed with high school and junior college students. I had been playing the violin for four years, loved it, and was so excited to participate with high school and junior college students in the string ensemble.

Then, the day before the concert, I was called into the principal's office. I was terrified, but could not think of a thing I had done. The news, however, devastated me. Giving no reason, he told me he was not going to allow me to get out of class for one hour to participate in the Christmas concert. In fact, he came and stood outside my classroom door to make sure I remained and did not join the concert ensemble.

My reaction, fueled by inner rage, led me to quit violin. My mother, who was sorry years later that she did nothing about this, was probably too consumed with her own grief to take up that battle. To this day, I cannot understand why someone would do something like that to an 8th grader who had a promising violin career in front of her. But the lack of any adult support—not my mom, not my violin teacher, not the choir director, and of course not my recently deceased father—was too much for me to handle.

On the one hand, I had deep enjoyment from learning to play the violin, and the accomplishment of advancing to play in a small string ensemble with much older students. On the other hand, I allowed a cruel action by an adult in power to discourage me from continuing. Today I enjoy the contrast of my violin experience with the experience in Suzuki violin lessons my granddaughter Elizabeth enjoys.

One of the things I relearned while serving in the state legislature is that there are always two sides to every story. At first blush, the story can look like a vast miscarriage of justice. On the other side, there are mitigating factors needing to be considered. So it is with life. Almost every down side has an up side. People have a good side and a not so good side. The astonishing thing is that God's grace covers everything, good and bad.

For a Bowl of Bean Soup

21 Because Rebecca had no children, Isaac prayed to the Lord for her. The Lord answered his prayer, and Rebecca became pregnant. 22 She was going to have twins, and before they were born, they struggled against each other in her womb. She said, "Why should something like this happen to me?" So she went to ask the Lord for an answer. 23 The Lord said to her, "Two nations are within you; You will give birth to two rival peoples. One will be stronger than the other; The older will serve the younger." 24 The time came for her to give birth, and she had twin sons. 25 The first one was reddish, and his skin was like a hairy robe, so he was named Esau. 26 The second one was born holding on tightly to the heel of Esau, so he was named Jacob. Isaac was sixty years old when they were born. 27 The boys grew up, and Esau became a skilled hunter, a man who loved the outdoors, but Jacob was a quiet man who stayed at home. 28 Isaac preferred Esau, because he enjoyed eating the animals Esau killed, but Rebecca preferred Jacob. 29 One day while Jacob was cooking some bean soup, Esau came in from hunting. He was hungry 30 and said to Jacob, "I'm starving; give me some of that red stuff." (That is why he was named Edom.) 31 Jacob answered, "I will give it to you if you give me your rights as the first-born son." 32 Esau said, "All right! I am about to die; what good will my rights do me?" 33 Jacob answered, "First make a vow that you will give me your rights." Esau made the vow and gave his rights to Jacob. 34 Then Jacob gave him some bread and some of the soup. He ate and drank and then got up and left. That was all Esau cared about his rights as the first-born son. Genesis 25:21-34

I have often felt a kinship with Esau. Not because he was born red and hairy as a furry robe, though I'm told that at birth I was as red as a sunburned nose and so hairy my father's neighbor asked him what kennel he picked me from. And my kinship with Esau is not even that he and I have the same passion and love for the out-of-doors racing through our arteries. Our kinship is much more elemental. Esau sold his birthright, his rights as the first-born son, his lion's share of the inheritance, his leadership of the clan, his special blessing from God. He traded all this for a lousy bowl of bean soup.

What does that have to do with me? What does that have to do with you? Not one of us would claim to be as foolish as Esau. If anything we might tie in more with Jacob, taking advantage of the situation to always get the best deal. But, no—we've got Esau in our chromosomes.

Like him, we're hungry, and to take care of the painful knot in the pit of our stomach, we're all too ready to put too much on the line, to let our life get out of whack, to slowly, gradually, one day at a time, one little step at a time, put our birthright on the block. The problem is that we are hungry and the soup smells fantastic.

My purpose is not to catalogue the trades or the sellouts for soup like the stockyard reports at the end of the day—500 hogs, 2000 head of cattle, 300 sheep, as many feeders. I know my own brokenness, my own tendencies to sell out, my own desire for bean soup at the expense of my birthright. I'm aware of the Esau that lurks within, and I suspect that you're aware of him inside of you, as well. We become like Esau whenever we put anything before our birthright.

But, hold on, you say, what is my birthright? So, lest we, like Esau, despise our gift, let us listen once again to some hauntingly simple words that point to that birthright.

"I baptize you in the name of the Father and the Son and the Holy Spirit." There's your birthright, there's your baptism in the Holy Spirit.

"For God so loved the world that he gave his only son, that whoever believes in him should not perish but have eternal life. For God did not send his son into the world to condemn the world, but that the world through him might be saved." Words from the Gospel of John.

"Peace I leave with you, my peace I give to you. Not as the world gives, do I give it unto you. Do not be worried, do not be afraid." Words of Jesus. There's your birthright.

"This is what love is; it is not that we have loved God, but that he loved us and sent his son to be the means by which our sins are forgiven. If God so loved us, then we should love one another." Words from 1st John.

There is your gift. There is a mission that would send adrenalin coursing through anyone's body. And that birthright is for us in our brokenness: *"O wretched man that I am! Who will deliver me from this body of death? But thanks be to God!"* Words of Paul.

"I believe that I cannot by my own reason or strength believe in Jesus Christ my Lord or come to him. But the Holy Spirit has called me through the Gospel." Words of Martin Luther. And we celebrate that birthright together: *"Our Lord Jesus Christ in the night he was betrayed, took bread, and when he had given thanks, he gave it to his disciples saying, 'take and eat. This is my body given for you.'"*

This is a feast that would make any ole bean soup this world could whip up pale in comparison.

Your birthright gives you an eye that goes beyond yourself and sees and burns for the injustice and hatred in this world. It empowers us to sacrifice ourselves for our brothers and sisters: *"For as much as you have done it to the least of these my brothers and sisters, you do it unto me."* Words of Jesus.

"I heard a loud voice speaking from the throne: 'Now God's home

is with mankind. He will live with them, and they shall be his people. God himself will be with them and he will be their God. He will wipe away every tear from their eyes. There will be no more death, no more grief, or crying or pain. The old things have disappeared. And now I make all things new."'

Our birthright points to a new existence promised to us: vision of John, Island of Patmos, the Book of Revelation.

You may be a praise-the-Lord, born again, baptized in the Spirit, praying, healing, tongues-speaking, turned-on charismatic with a "Jesus saves" button in your lapel and a "ONE WAY" bumper sticker on your guitar case. Or you may be an icy cold professor of good Scandinavian stock, filled with Kierkegaardian angst, subject to fits of existential paralysis, depression and naval gazing, riddled with doubts about the meaning of your life and faith.

But know this: You've been given a birthright: Jesus Christ, God's Son, our Savior. Born in a barn and raised of common folk, he suffered, died, was raised, and is present, moving and working in power among and within us. Jesus Christ, Jesus Christ, Jesus Christ!

Reflection

Contemplating this sermon, never having thought much about the story of Esau and Jacob, except to think Esau was shortsighted to sell his birthright for a bowl of bean soup, I see the connection between Esau and us, between his birthright and ours, and it amazes me.

Mark writes about his tendency to sell out and put his own desires before God's gift of blessing. I share that tendency in many ways. I like my life to be comfortable and to surround myself with my favorite things—an easy path to follow.

On the other hand, sometimes we plunge into something, not

knowing if we are opting for a bowl of bean soup or claiming our birthright. On the eve of my 60th birthday, and newly retired from my all-encompassing job of coaching, I came up with a crazy idea to challenge myself physically and, as it turned out, emotionally and spiritually.

Filled with a sense of adventure, I had a desire to buy a good bike and to ride my age with a zero on the end (yes, that would be 600 miles). Alone. In addition, the ride was to include four states and visits at as many Good Samaritan nursing homes as I could along the way. After all, I was a new member of the Good Samaritan National Board of Directors, and I thought it would be unique to visit their facilities on my bicycle. Mark Dickerson, the public affairs director, helped put my route together and let the facilities know I would be coming.

After riding 75 miles to Scotland, South Dakota, on the first day, and fighting a west wind most of the afternoon, I bedded down in a not so comfy nursing home bed that had been wheeled into the administrator's office. At least I had a place to sleep for the night. I remember calling Mike and Kelly and reporting on experiencing minute-by-minute misery as the afternoon wore on and I rode many more miles than I was used to, while a newly-acquired head cold had turned my nose into a faucet.

The next morning I went shopping for some sweet rolls for my new best friends from the previous night's dinner—nursing home residents who reported a shortage of such items. And then it was off to Wagner for lunch with the advisory board and administrator. I fought that same pesky wind and was a bit late for the lunch meeting. As I entered the town, a woman just leaving pulled over on the side, zipped down her window, and said, "Are you from Sioux Falls?" "I am," I said brightly. "Well, they're waiting for you!" she sputtered and sped off.

Michelle Juffers, the administrator, welcomed me to the nursing home and to a much-appreciated lunch. After lunch and a tour, Michelle said she was worried that I was going to try to make it to O'Neill, Nebraska, by nightfall. She gave me the numbers of her two brothers who lived there, emphasizing that they would be happy to come and get me if I needed their assistance.

With Howard Bisch, advisory board member and avid cyclist helping break the wind for the first nine miles, I naively set out. After navigating a steep downhill to Pickstown, nearly crashing as the gusty wind increased at times to 35 miles per hour, I crossed the Missouri and faced the first of multiple, long, steep uphill climbs. The wind provided constant push back, daring me to continue. When I finally turned south toward O'Neill and had the wind with me, I thought I had it made.

Not so fast, pronounced a narrow, hilly road with skinny bridges. One semi-truck passed me close enough to reach out and touch it, and the wind stream nearly forced me into the river. When I arrived in Spencer, with the afternoon sun rapidly descending, I again thought I would make my destination, and pulled out my cell phone to make contact with Michelle's brothers. Silly me, thinking there would be cell phone service out there.

Way too fast, the sun sank behind the horizon, and darkness began to gather. Realizing I had no options, I fought exhaustion as I peddled beyond 100 miles. Traffic was light, and a pickup truck coming toward me at least made me feel I was not all alone on the highway. Suddenly the pickup did a U-turn behind me, pulled in front of me, and stopped. A large black dog looked at me curiously. The driver got out and came toward me.

By this time, my fatigue made me immune to fear, and all I could think of was a ride to town with, I hoped, one of Michelle's brothers. And it was one of the brothers, who quickly loaded my bike in the truck while I managed to climb onto the seat. He took me home with him, got my bed ready, and ordered in a chicken dinner for us from a local restaurant, undoubtedly the best meal I have tasted in my life. An angel with a dog in a pick-up!

An entry in my journal that evening said: "Learning how great people are to help; how good it is to challenge self, get out of the comfort zone, be alone." The adventures continued as I peddled east to my next destination, a nursing home in Bloomfield, Nebraska. From there it was on to Sioux City and north to Storm Lake, Iowa, and a welcome and much-needed stay with my long-time friend, Marge Willadsen, a coach and professor at Buena Vista University.

Physically and even to some degree psychologically, I have never experienced a more difficult time in my life. It was lonely on the road, especially in western South Dakota and Nebraska. Body parts ached and begged not to be used again: my butt, my shoulders, my wrists and hands, my feet. The fatigue that set in later in the day was mind numbing.

Before I even left my garage, I was worried about safety on the road and the real possibility of not seeing my family again. The roads in Iowa were the worst. Going east from Sioux City, the highway was narrow and hilly. Big semis were unable to swing out much because the driver never knew what was coming over the next hill.

Once I had to ride onto the shoulder and quickly discovered that was a bad move. The loose rocks tipped my bike back onto the road, and, in a panic, I crawled off the highway, dragging my bike behind me. A driver behind me stopped to make sure I was OK. I tried to smile and say I was OK, and that I just needed to blow my nose (I had a horrendous cold during the entire ride). He took one look at the snot coming out of my nose and took off.

On the ride from Storm Lake, Iowa, to Estherville, a strong, cold north wind picked up as the day went on, increasing to 25 or 30 miles per hour at times. It slowed me, sapping my energy.

About 3 p.m. I stopped at a gas station in a small town. After a small snack, I asked the woman who was the proprietor how much farther it was to Estherville.

"32 miles," she said, "and you better peddle fast."

I used this advice to motivate myself when I started slowing down. It was so dark I could barely see as I rode into Estherville, and snowflakes had started falling.

The temperature dropped from 80 degrees the first two days to 23 degrees as I left my sixth overnight in a nursing home in Estherville, Iowa.

Finally, I was headed west, and adrenalin surged as I anticipated getting home after my last stay in Luverne, Minnesota. The trip planner had me taking I-90 from Jackson, Minnesota, to Sioux Falls, but I thought I remembered Minnesota did not allow bicycles on interstates. My intuition was verified a few miles west of Worthington, when a loud siren rudely interrupted the music from my iPod.

A friendly and efficient sheriff helped me load my bike into her car and quickly deposited me on a county road—with no ticket. The side road afforded a quiet relief from the noise of the interstate highways, and I made it to Luverne just as twilight brought chillier temperatures.

The stay in the nursing home in Luverne was memorable. Besides the joy of friends meeting me in the evening and the morning, I witnessed love in action by a certified nursing assistant. Since I shared a bathroom with my next-door neighbor, I could easily hear the conversation between her and the nursing assistant, as she got ready for the day.

She was new and worried about her situation. The early-morning conversation was a litany of love as the assistant answered her often-repeated questions patiently and with compassion.

For five nights, a nursing home was my home away from home. I toured each home, talked with staff and residents, and took a shower down the hall where the residents are bathed. Comfortable and private it was not, but I got a great look at those nursing homes and the people who lived there as well as the staff, a vision that inspired me.

As Mark testified, all of us have times when we let our lives get out of whack, gradually, one day at a time, putting our birthright on the block. What a good thing that God keeps calling us back and reminding us we are his children.

My encounters with close calls on the road, nursing home residents and administrators, and people I met along the way became these spiritual reminders. The journey was a gift, an experience that deepened my faith, and took me beyond myself, while challenging my fears and physical abilities. God reminded me again and again that he is my constant companion, providing protection and help when I need it, and that ultimately he alone enables me to claim my birthright—God's blessing of faith and forgiveness through our Lord.

P. S.

1 After this, Jesus appeared once more to his disciples at Lake Tiberias. This is how it happened. 2 Simon Peter, Thomas (called the Twin), Nathanael (the one from Cana in Galilee), the sons of Zebedee, and two other disciples of Jesus were all together. 3 Simon Peter said to the others, "I am going fishing." "We will come with you," they told him. So they went out in a boat, but all that night they did not catch a thing. 4 As the sun was rising, Jesus stood at the water's edge, but the disciples did not know that it was Jesus. 5 Then he asked them, "Young men, haven't you caught anything?" "Not a thing," they answered. 6 He said to them, "Throw your net out on the right side of the boat, and you will catch some." So they threw the net out and could not pull it back in, because they had caught so many fish. 7 The disciple whom Jesus loved said to Peter, "It is the Lord!" When Peter heard that it was the Lord, he wrapped his outer garment around him (for he had taken his clothes off) and jumped into the water. 8 The other disciples came to shore in the boat, pulling the net full of fish. They were not very far from land, about a hundred yards away. 9 When they stepped ashore, they saw a charcoal fire there with fish on it and some bread. 10 Then Jesus said to them, "Bring some of the fish you have just caught." 11 Simon Peter went aboard and dragged the net ashore full of big fish, a hundred and fifty-three in all; even though there were so many, still the net did not tear. 12 Jesus said to them, "Come and eat." None of the disciples dared ask him, "Who are you?" because they knew it was the Lord. 13 So Jesus went over, took the bread, and gave it to them; he did the same with the fish. 14 This, then, was the third time Jesus appeared to the disciples after he was raised from death. 15 After they had eaten, Jesus said to Simon Peter, "Simon son of John, do you love me more than these others do?" "Yes, Lord," he answered, "you know that I love you." Jesus said to him, "Take care of my lambs." 16 A second time Jesus said to him, "Simon son of John, do you love me?" "Yes, Lord," he answered, "you know that I love you." Jesus said to him, "Take care of my sheep." 17 A third time Jesus said, "Simon son of John, do you love me?" Peter became sad because Jesus asked him the third time, "Do you love me?" and so he said to him, "Lord, you know everything; you know that I love you!" Jesus said to him, "Take care of my sheep. 18 I am telling you the truth: when you were young, you used to get ready and go anywhere you wanted to; but when you are old, you will stretch out your hands and someone else will tie you up and take you where you don't want to go." 19 (In saying this, Jesus was indicating the way in which Peter would die and bring glory to God.) Then Jesus said to him, "Follow me!" 20 Peter turned around and saw behind him that other disciple, whom Jesus loved—the one who had leaned close to Jesus at the meal and had asked, "Lord, who is going to betray you?" 21 When Peter saw him, he asked Jesus, "Lord, what about this man?" 22 Jesus answered him, "If I want him to live until I come, what is that to you? Follow me!" John 21:1-19

I love postscripts—a little P.S. at the end. When I think of my life, I think that some of the most significant events I have experienced have been punctuated by P. S. We see postscripts everywhere. On a tombstone, we call them an epitaph—a little postscript to a person's life. One woman had written on hers—"See, I told you I was sick!" In my own life, some of the most significant postscripts have also been the most unexpected. I remember being a junior in college, twenty years old, and receiving a letter from my father. It was just a nice, newsy little note, and then there was a postscript. It said, P. S.

P. S.

Your mother is pregnant. What a postscript!

Sandy and I had been struggling in our relationship during those years in college, and after a long, late-night discussion, she gave me a letter. I will never forget the P.S. She wrote: "P. S. Even though my feelings aren't there, I want to spend the rest of my life with you. I am yours with a will to love." That P. S. opened up our relationship in a way nothing else had, and not long after, we were engaged. Our love for each other has only grown and deepened since that day.

The Gospel of John ended with these words from the end of chapter 20, verse 30: *These are written that you might believe that Jesus is the Christ, the Son of God, and believing, have life in his name.* Done.

And then the writer started to do a little thinking and musing about that story. Somewhere later on, he decided to pen a postscript for us. We call it chapter 21. That postscript actually has two events, one that leads into the next. The first fourteen verses of chapter 21 take place in a beautiful little setting by the Sea of Galilee, which we call Lake Tiberius. The camera focuses in on this setting, and we see it in broad, panoramic scope.

Narrowing further, it focuses on two people, Jesus and Peter, in verses 15 to 22, which is the end of John's Gospel. We have that marvelous little sharing, where Jesus asks Peter, *"Peter, do you love me?"* You remember that. But the first part of that postscript, for us, is this incident of seven disciples making contact with the risen Lord. The writer calls it the third resurrection appearance.

Why did he pen that postscript? What does it have to say to us? I suspect we will never know why, and perhaps that is not so important. But what it does to his early readers and hearers, and what it does to us, is a phenomenal gift. It reminds us again of the importance of the resurrection for those disciples and for us, his disciples. From that text, we see three powerful ways in which his appearance, as the resurrected Lord, radically changes our life, does something to us. Think of the context in which this took place. Not the lake side context, but the immediate context. Jesus Christ was killed, and then, through the eyes of faith and a couple of experiences, but still perceived and finally trusted in faith, he was raised.

The whole milieu was one of death. Not just because of the death of Jesus, but also because of the time. Those times around the life of Jesus were filled with death. To see people nailed on crosses, hanging there, was a common sight for all people. Public executions were frequent. At the time the Gospel of John was penned, and this postscript was written, executions were part and parcel of everyday life as they have been in Israel today, with suicide bombers everywhere.

Not like us. Most of the time we do not experience death. So, when someone we love dies, death grabs us and shakes up our life. In a lot of ways, our culture denies death, we soft-pedal it, we soften it. No soft-pedaling for them. Death was a harsh reality, and so this postscript was penned.

This postscript gave hope in the face of death to its readers. Jesus Christ was raised. He appeared to his disciples. He spoke with them. He interacted with them. He had been dead, really dead, and was brought back to life. He took those seven disciples, who were with him, and again funneled a laser beam of hope into their lives when they thought about death. And to that early Church, which, during the time this was written, had death all around, it gave hope again in the face of death. What a gift!

We in our community experience death often, even though we try to deny it and masquerade it. Death is a part of our life. Many of you could tell stories that would make us sad, stories about the reality of death you have experienced. But we also have this word of hope. Jesus Christ was raised from the dead. His is the first fruits, as Paul says, for all who would believe. The promise that we have, for us and for those whom we love, for all believers, is hope. What a delightful little P. S.

Second, this was penned for us and for those disciples in that early Church, to help us all see that the resurrection of Jesus Christ radically changed the ordinary, humdrum, day-to-day kind of life. "Well," Peter said, "I'm going fishing." You know, it was his old job. The rest said, "I'm coming along." All night long they fished. No luck. And then you remember the story: In the morning, the mist is rising on the lake. They see a figure, and they do not know who it is. He calls out to them, "Any luck?" They say no. "Throw your nets down on the deep side." They do. And the nets are overwhelmed. Common, day-to-day ordinary experiences suddenly radically transformed. There were so many fish they were unable even pull them into the boat. They had to drag them along behind the boat to get them into shore. What a radical change!

The resurrection of Jesus Christ does the same kind of thing for us. His power and his presence change the way we perceive and, therefore, experience all of life. How easy it is for us to see things as we sometimes think they exist. We get up in the morning, grab a shower and get ready for the day. We go to work oblivious of God's presence in our daily lives. But the resurrection of Jesus Christ and his presence in the midst of his people, through word, through sacrament, through his Spirit, in the context of a believing community where two or three are gathered together in his name, radically changes all of life.

We begin to see life in a different way. We see meaning in the day-to-day and in the ordinary. Transformed by him, we experience each conversation we have, each relationship, each encounter with another, as not simply a bumping into another, but as a sacred and holy event. Open to that reality, who knows what can happen, and how life can change?

I walked into the hospital room a couple of days ago to visit an older woman, struggling with cancer. And my fantasy of what it would be like was that it would be a nice little hospital visit, like pastors make. But in that hospital room the power of God's Spirit, the presence of Christ, was there. The sharing and the give and take that happened were only and could only be described as a gift from God. The tears and the love, the forgiveness and the hope, that took place were a marvelous gift for both of us. That kind of transformation is for you, in your cars as you drive home, with your spouse, your kids. Jesus Christ enters into our life and gives meaning to our existence. A marvelous P. S.

The power of Jesus Christ, the resurrected Lord, touches us in the midst of our failures. We think of what it was like. They were out there pulling in the fish, when the huge catch suddenly opened up the eyes of the beloved disciple and he said, *"It is the Lord!"* Peter wrapped himself quickly around with his outer garment, jumped into the water and swam to shore.

Remember Peter and the events leading to the crucifixion? Remember how, with a big, broad stroke and bold words, he said, *"Lord, though everyone else leaves you, I will never deny you."* Jesus said, *"Three times you will deny me before the cock crows twice."* And he did. We are told, when Jesus saw him, Peter left and wept bitterly. Now, with that kind of past, to see Jesus again on the shore, one would be ashamed. Wouldn't you? I would. One would think, I'm going to lay back. I'm going to hide in the crew or think of some kind of an excuse. But the presence of the resurrected Christ did something to Peter. The love that flowed from Christ pulled him out of the boat, into the water so he could be there with Christ. He couldn't even wait for the boat to come in—he had to be with his Lord right now!

This is such good news. I would say, the one thing I see in us, more than almost anything else, is the struggle we constantly work with in terms of our own failures. We are all afraid of failure. When I talk with students in my office, one of the things that we talk about is what are you afraid of, and the thing that comes up again and again is, "I'm afraid of failure." So we always cover our tracks, leave a little back door, an excuse. "You know, I didn't do well, but I really didn't study. If I had studied I would have done well..."

In our relationships or in our life goals, we dream pea-sized, shriveled-up dreams. We are afraid to dream the big ones, because we fear failure. So we don't risk, we don't step out, we don't launch out. Failure.

We take a look at our lives, and we see a trail of broken and empty promises that are part of our existence. We feel guilty, it bothers us to look at it again, so we stuff it down and pretend that life goes on as it normally does. Yet, it haunts us, whether as pastor, as student, as parent. No matter who we are, what haunts us is that shadow of our brokenness and of our failure.

Jesus is not repulsed by the dark side of our being, not turned off by our failures. He grants us forgiveness, reaches out for us, and gives us the strength to launch out, living in the freedom of forgiveness. He calls us to risk, to share, and to feed his sheep, his lambs. "Lord, you know that I love You." "Feed my sheep." What a postscript. What power for us.

This whole story, this postscript, is in a setting that is enshrouded in mystery. If you have been up early in the morning at a lake when mist is on the water, you know how distances are distorted, shapes come and go, and familiar sights appear mysterious.

In the same way, that appearance and the resurrection of our Lord Jesus Christ is a mystery to us, beyond our rational comprehension. Another world penetrates ours and is yet so far beyond it. But the power is there, the reality is there, brilliantly, for us to see, to struggle with, to experience. We walk by faith and not by sight.

That postscript, mysterious, beautiful, powerful, is written to you. The invitation is to apprehend it by faith, to trust that God is present in our dying and in our death, and beyond. We are called to trust that he is here in the seemingly small encounters of day-to-day life, filling them with meaning. He invites us to risk, to trust that our sins are indeed forgiven, that our failures are forgotten, that the freedom of our future is one that God invites us to step into as we step into the mist, knowing that Jesus Christ is there, resurrected for us, with us, loving us.

Finally, that P. S. could be summed up in just a few words. It could be summed up: "P. S. All my children, I love you."

Reflection

So faith is a gift. We cannot do anything to achieve it on our own. Have you ever wondered if you have it? Got milk? Got faith? I have spent a lifetime wondering, hoping I do, but doubt creeps in. God knows when that happens and provides me with real-life experiences to still that voice of doubt. My recovery from being kicked in the stomach by a horse and having my liver split wide open is one of those miracles. God should never have to repeat his promise to be with us after something like that happens, but just like the Israelites in the wilderness kept going astray every time Moses retreated to speak with God, we, too, go astray and need reminders of God's faithfulness to us, and God's gift of faith.

I had more than one reminder of God's faithfulness after Mark died. And I needed as many reminders as I could get! Irrational thoughts and fears would come over me the winter Mark died, like: It's so cold outside. He must be so cold in his grave! Fear and anxiety and grief wanted to chase faith away.

But a story came my way, told from one person to the next

until I got it, the old-fashioned way. It was about Bob, a man who lived in International Falls and had been a loyal parishioner in our church. He had seven children, one of whom Mark helped ordain into the ministry. Bob had become ill and was about to have heart surgery. He was terrified, the story went. But then Mark appeared to him in a vision and assured him everything was going to be fine. He calmed right down, had surgery, and woke up to begin his next lease on life.

Another story: It was a sunny spring day, and I had to go out to the airport, about six miles away, to get my ticket changed for a trip. I decided to ride my bicycle to get some exercise at the same time. My route led me along the Sioux River bike trail, a pleasant ride accompanied by sand pipers, robins, and Canadian geese. When I arrived at the airport, I wheeled my bike through the doors and went up to the counter. A helpful young woman got me the perfect spot on my future flight.

Meanwhile, at the next counter, Mike, a handsome young man I had known since he was a student at Augustana, greeted me. He wanted to talk. I told him I would be right over as soon as I was finished. In a few moments, new ticket in hand, I wheeled my bike over to Mike's counter. He was working the counter for one of the airlines that day. No one else was at the counter, behind the counter, or anywhere near the counter, and it remained that way, oddly enough, for the next twenty-five minutes, the time it took for Mike to share his story. It was just Mike, me, and my bike.

"When did Mark die?" he asked. I told him it was the evening of March 29, about 8 p.m., the Saturday before Easter that year. He proceeded to tell me about his close relationship with his father, who grew up in Turkey, and how he had died. He said the night after Mark died He had awakened shortly after midnight, and felt someone was in the room. He thought it might be the spirit of his father, and called out to him. Instead, Mark's figure appeared in the room, smiling, telling him his father was safe.

We both stood at the ticket counter in the Sioux Falls airport with tears streaming down our cheeks. Still, no customer or airline employee was anywhere in sight. Finally, I wheeled my bike outside and peddled home, grateful for the miraculous story Mike had shared with me.

Why Mike? Why Bob? Perhaps because they had had faith-filled talks with Mark. Perhaps the story would be shared with their families in a helpful way. I have no idea why. But I am extremely grateful those stories were shared with me, banishing the doubts that sometimes take over.

P. S. Don't worry. Everything will be fine. I love you.

The Rest of the Story

3 We also boast of our troubles, because we know that trouble produces endurance, 4 endurance brings God's approval, and his approval creates hope. 5 This hope does not disappoint us, for God has poured out his love into our hearts by means of the Holy Spirit, who is God's gift to us. Romans 5:3-5

There are little things that I like to listen to when I get a chance. One of them makes my ears perk up like a deer in the woods when someone steps on a stick. I am listening to the radio, absorbed in a story, and then, at the most suspenseful time, the station takes a commercial break, but I hear Paul Harvey say that in a minute he will tell "the rest of the story." I wait. I hope. I can't resist listening. You have heard Paul Harvey, haven't you? That well-known radio personality who relays fascinating little vignettes and then teases the listener by throwing in a commercial before the often-surprising "rest of the story."

One night I was in a great mood, and my kids noticed it. My young daughter Sarah said to me, "Daddy, if I told you something that happened a long time ago, would you be mad now?"

Her softness and goodness melted me down to my toes, and I said, "No."

"Well," she said, "do you remember that time last year when I fell down the steps, and I got all bloody and I had to stay home from school for half a day?"

"Yes, I remember," I said. How could I forget?!

"Well," she said, "actually I didn't really fall down the stairs." She said, "I was sliding down the railing frontward and I let go."

Pow! And there I had the rest of the story!

Now, the Gospel of Jesus Christ intrigues us, because there is always an element to it of "the rest of the story." It has to do with us. It reminds me of those tacky T-shirts that have a gem of truth in them: Be patient, God is not finished with me yet. The rest of the story...

Something about the Gospel comes at us from our future and explodes into our very present, changing all that is now. And that rest of the story is called "hope." *"Endurance brings God's approval, and his approval creates hope. And this hope does not disappoint us."*

The rest of our story is a delight and a gift. It changes us.

During World War II, in Norway, high in the mountains at the end of a fjord is a little village. This village, like the rest of Norway, had been under the domination of Germany, and the whole village lived under the pall that hung over them. But the war was over; the Allies had won. Norway was again free.

However, word did not get to that little village. And so, though they were free, they lived as though they were not. They lived as if in slavery. Then, months later, communication finally got through to the village: "You are free!" With that word, lives were radically changed, because now they knew.

From our future comes a word to our present to tell us that we are free. The victory has been won. We are forgiven. We are loved. Life, that great gift, has been bestowed upon us. Now that we have been put right with God through faith, we have peace with God through our Lord Jesus Christ. There for you is the rest of the story.

That should change the way we live!

That should change the way that we look at ourselves. It should help us to accept ourselves, to forgive ourselves, to love ourselves.

And that should make us grateful for growth, grateful for change.

God is not finished with us yet. For us, there is the rest of the story. I think of all those who are on their way in life, perhaps just starting out, or perhaps somewhere in the middle, and I marvel at where God may lead them, may lead you.

The rest of the story. It changes the way we relate to one another. It helps us to judge not ourselves or others, if we accept that things are not finished yet. Those critical attitudes we have might be radically changed when we get beneath the surface in a relationship and see a deep and hurting and very real person. A bond of friendship that is genuine and life giving can then be created.

The rest of the story. It does something to us in terms of the way we look at our world. Trouble, war, famine, and natural disasters are everywhere, but the story is not complete. That chapter has not been written yet. We have an opportunity to right those wrongs, to take part in the rest of the story for our world, to dig into the problems, to deal with them efficiently, effectively and with passion. Our task is to bring mercy and justice into this world in the name of Jesus Christ. There is power here. And hope.

He went to St. Olaf College. He was a troublemaker, he was rebellious, he was a pastor's son, and he had a reputation that would not quit. After four years, he did not have the grades to graduate. All his classmates were getting ready, trying on their black robes in order to march in the parade to receive their diploma from President Clemens Granskou. Sunday afternoon, an hour before commencement was to begin, Clemens Granskou picked up the phone and called that rebellious student and said, "Come into my office. I want to talk to you."

Trembling, he walked through the door. Granskou said to him, "Look over there." Hanging in the corner was a black robe and a square hat. He said, "Try it on. It's your size. It's for you. Now get out of here. The next time I will see you is when I shake your hand and give you your diploma."

Let me tell you the rest of the story. The rebellious student was a man named Fritz Norstad. He was so moved by that gift, that affirmation of himself in spite of everything else, that he went on to the seminary, went on beyond that and got a doctorate. He then established in Chicago what is called the Institute of Human Ecology at Lutheran General Hospital. Through that institute, troubled people from all over the world have been helped and have been given new hope and a new life. Now you know the rest of the story.

Endurance creates approval from God. And that approval produces hope. And that hope will not disappoint us. And you can look forward to the rest of your story.

Reflection

Sarah's little revelation about what really happened to her when she had her accident, taking advantage of Mark's great mood, is mild compared to the stories parents hear later on when the kids are grown and decide to share some of what really happened at home when the parents were not around. I have heard a few of those quite recently from my adult children.

Mark, since he was a pastor's kid, tried to look like he was a rebel, rolling his cigarettes up in his T-shirt sleeve and growing his hair. Later on, when he was a pastor in International Falls he even added a motorcycle and a leather vest.

I laughed at everything except the motorcycle. After one ride with him, I assailed him at every opportunity until he got rid of it. My brother was killed on a motorcycle while in the Navy stationed on the island of Guam, so my opinion of motorcycles is consistent with my daughter Rachel's opinion: they are donor-cycles.

A little innocent-looking book perches on my fireplace mantel entitled, *How Did I Get Here so Fast?* The reference is to old age, which is looking alarmingly close. I find myself giving illustrations to people that begin, "Back in the dark ages when I was young…"

In some ways it does feel like a very long time ago—a different century even! As I rewind the clock and review some of the unexpected things that happened in my life, I compile the rest of my story.

I grew up in a time and place that valued women as wives, lovers, mothers, and homemakers. To make a little money while you were waiting to get married, women were teachers, secretaries or nurses. Since both my parents were college educated, which was highly unusual back then, I expected and planned to go to college and graduate. I expected to find a husband and get married and have a family. That was it.

I am a goal-driven person, and I am a bit shocked as I look back on my life's dreams. But I got lucky because I was persistent in telling my mother that St. Olaf was my destiny. I began and finished college in three and a half years. In between was the answer to prayer, a man I fell in love with, who returned that love.

So I did the usual thing and taught to put my husband through the seminary. During his post-graduate studies at Union Seminary in Richmond, Virginia, we welcomed our first child, Rachel. Two years later our son, Michael, was born, followed quickly by Sarah. From teacher to mom and homemaker. I loved those children, but with Mark working seven days a week and many nights, I was lonely. The eternal winter of International Falls and short days with little daylight did not help matters. Thank heaven for Pat and Ruby and Audrey.

My life opened up when we moved to Sioux Falls, and I was recruited to coach women's softball at Augustana College. This led to two advanced degrees, never in the plan, a full-time job, and coaching 39 teams over 27 years. I feel fortunate to have had all the experiences and opportunities that life has opened up for me and a husband who encouraged me to pursue advanced degrees and work full-time in a venue I loved.

After stepping down from my full-time job I continued to teach part-time at Augustana, and then found myself recruited to run for the state legislature. Being in the legislature was, as my friend Bill Thompson used to say, the best graduate school I could attend—and a fascinating and frustrating growing experience. Although I campaigned to win, I have no regrets about not being in the Senate this time around. I did my best, worked as hard as I could all year long, and am grateful for the people I met, the friends I made, and the experiences I encountered.

Looking back on my life and how things played out, I feel as if someone shuffled the cards for me. But the one thing I regret is that the rest of my story does not include having Mark around. I can only imagine how much fun we would be having sharing the rest of our stories together.

Thinking about Thinking

8 In conclusion, my friends, fill your minds with those things that are good and that deserve praise: things that are true, noble, right, pure, lovely, and honorable. 9 Put into practice what you learned and received from me, both from my words and from my actions. And the God who gives us peace will be with you. Philippians 4:8-9.

Oh God, we think of your constant love. Psalm 48:9. Now, what do you think? Matthew 21:28.

One of the best signs I've ever seen was put over a parking space, and it said: "Don't you ever even think about parking in this space!"

Let's think for a moment about thinking. What do you fill your mind with? If someone were to step into your mind and take a look around, what would he or she see? What do you think about? To be sure, a lot of our thinking is determined and bubbles up deep from within from our subconscious, and many would argue whether or not we have control over this kind of thinking. Some of our greatest creative urges and our most shameful thoughts and feelings seem to creep up to the top, sometimes with great joy, sometimes like leaking sewer gas.

What do you think about? What do you fill up your mind with? I have a hunch that many of us are lazy, slothful thinkers, and that we fill our minds with whatever comes along. "What am I going to wear this morning?" "Who am I going to get together with after work?" "What do I have to do to get that person to like me?" Our minds become a racetrack for little things that chase here and there and bump into each other all the time. I suspect all of us fill our minds with some of that—we have to keep going, after all, during the day.

What do you fill your mind with? What do you think about? There are those times when our minds are cluttered, and we find ourselves guilty of mind pollution. At times our minds become a *tabula rasa* for anything that comes along and becomes attached like barnacles to the hull of a ship. We open ourselves up to a lot of garbage. We read and look at trash. We stare at the TV, and our eyes begin to get as square as the box we look at, uncritically, just to pass time. We'd rather read Playboy than study Picasso. Our minds are polluted with a lot of junk, harboring thoughts and plots that stem from our ruminating about resentments we hang onto, anger that goes unabated, unchallenged and un-confronted, fears that grip us, loneliness, despair, discouragement—a whole host of things flood our mind and determine, in large part, who we are and what we do.

And what don't we think about? What don't we fill our minds with? Here in our little communities we can become so provincial that we cease to struggle with the great, sensitive, ethical issues of our age, and we cease to do more than give a fleeting glance to concerns that each of us should be radically involved with. These are fundamental issues of our world: nuclear disarmament; how to alleviate hunger worldwide; how to move toward protecting our world, its air, water, animals, and natural resources, from greed and destruction. What don't we think of? What is *not* going on inside this space we call our minds? What do we fail to fill it up with?

Perhaps for all of us here, we need to pause for a moment and think about our thinking—really examine what goes on in our minds. And maybe we have to have the courage to do some cutting. The novelist Petr Dimitru writes in one of his little stories about a place in Germany where, high in the mountains, a lot of logging goes on. Through the years, they have built big wooden chutes. After they cut down the trees high in the mountain, they shoot the logs down, literally for thousands of feet, to where they can be skidded out of the woods and taken to lumber mills. These chutes are well used, not only with logs, but also with the loggers who will hop on and go tobogganing down to save them that long walk.

He tells of one logger who got his foot caught in that chute. As he was trying to work it loose, he heard a call from on top of the mountain warning that a log was coming down in case anyone was on the chute. Frantically he tried to pull himself free, but could not. So he took his ax and hacked away at his leg, cutting off his foot just in time to jump from the chute before the log rumbled by. The novelist tells us that he lived the rest of his life a cripple, but at least he was alive.

When we examine what our thinking, and that which directs our life, is all about, perhaps we are called to have the courage to cut. Perhaps we need to cut out some of the thinking habits we have fallen into. Perhaps we need to let go of those secret resentments, plots, ill will, bad feelings, and do as St. Paul invites us to do: *"Fill your minds with those things that are good and that deserve praise, things that are true, noble right, pure, lovely, and honorable."* We have some control over what we think about. Paul invites us to think about things that are good—good in the eyes of our Lord, good for ourselves, good for our community, for one another. Listen to him! Use your life and the gift of your intellect to struggle, to think, and to fill your mind with those good, honorable, pure, wise, important issues and perspectives. It will help to make you into the person you were created to be through the strength of our Lord Jesus Christ.

Reflection

I feel convicted! This sermon was a bulls-eye for me. Many times a day I allow my mind to wander, and it often is attracted to negative places, like an ex-smoker looking for a cigarette. I rework old problems or replay the past as I try to invoke an alternate conclusion. Sometimes I even rewind softball games and think what I could have done differently as a coach to facilitate a different ending. I apply that unsavory thinking to relationships, worrying about what I said or did, or what someone else said or did. The point is, such thinking is worthless meandering. Although we may be able to learn from the past, we cannot change it. I know life is lived in the present moment, and I try to remind myself of that again and again. It takes discipline and repetition. Kind of reminds me of coaching or teaching or parenting.

As a coach, one thing I stressed to my players was the importance of focus. It sounds elementary to say to players at that level, "Just watch the ball," but that is often the thing that is most easily forgotten. Players are often chewing themselves out for a past mistake or thinking about what they will do to redeem themselves in the future instead of staying focused on the moment. My years of coaching totaled 27, but I coached 39 seasons of teams due to being a dual sport head coach for 12 years. Although I gave up coaching in 2003, as in parenting, one is never finished.

Today I sat around a table in the basement of a church with several of my former student athletes having a deeply focused conversation about life and death. One of our teammates, Kim Kouri, had lost her father, and we were there to express our love and support. Many of my former student athletes have gone into coaching and then on to other venues. One, Kim Sudbeck, was asked if she missed coaching. She said she loved and missed planning and executing practices, the competitions, and the traveling. We agreed that we did not miss the fund-raising and recruiting. The mind of a successful coach is focused like a laser, always devising better ways of recruiting, practicing, or playing. It keeps one sharp, but over time it also slowly saps one's energy.

I have been asked countless times whether or not I miss coaching. I describe my feelings as one who has been at a great banquet and feasted on all the entrées and probably had four desserts. I am fully satisfied. 39 seasons of coaching competitive college women in one of the top conferences in the nation in Division II athletics is just right. I do miss the close relationships developed with the student athletes, but then I often connect with many of them.

Now that I have more time in my life, the opportunities for my mind to wander down unproductive paths are more frequent. I keep reminding myself to stay in the present and to enjoy the little moments. Last week I was part of the grandma task force to care for Mike and Kelly's four children while they took some important time away for themselves. The opportunity to really focus on precious moments was a gift.

The first night I sat down with four-year-old Luke to listen to his cello songs. It was dark outside, and the soft light in the living room illumined an irresistibly cute but serious boy, as he removed the cello from the case, let the stand out and tightened it carefully, and got a grip on the bow. It was the first time I had heard him play, and I loved it. Later that evening I slipped into bed with seven-year-old Elizabeth, and, in the darkness of her bedroom, wove a story around the two stars that shone from the walls. After I thought I had told a wonderful story and actually thought about writing it up, Elizabeth said, "I'm still awake." But a few minutes of a back rub took care of that. In the morning, I held 19-month old Christian in my lap at the kitchen table while reading a story that both Elizabeth and he enjoyed as they were eating their Cheerios.

Just live in the moment, be here now. Banish negative or even positive thoughts of the past. Embrace today and the people you meet. When your mind wanders, whether in prayer or at other times, gently bring it back. Think of the gifts, big and little, that God has placed in your life. *Put into practice what you learned and received from me, both from my words and from my actions. And the God who gives us peace will be with you* (Philippians 4:8-9).

Change

21 Jesus and his disciples came to the town of Capernaum, and on the next Sabbath Jesus went to the synagogue and began to teach. 22 The people who heard him were amazed at the way he taught, for he wasn't like the teachers of the Law; instead, he taught with authority. 23 Just then a man with an evil spirit came into the synagogue and screamed, 24 "What do you want with us, Jesus of Nazareth? Are you here to destroy us? I know who you are—you are God's holy messenger!" 25 Jesus ordered the spirit, "Be quiet, and come out of the man!" 26 The evil spirit shook the man hard, gave a loud scream, and came out of him. 27 The people were all so amazed that they started saying to one another, "What is this? Is it some kind of new teaching? This man has authority to give orders to the evil spirits, and they obey him!" 28 And so the news about Jesus spread quickly everywhere in the province of Galilee. Mark 1:21-28*

My wife Sandy and I were in the beautiful village in Capernaum where this story takes place. We walked into a gorgeous garden with flowers of every hue. Beyond the garden gate, we discovered the ruins of what had once been a small village. To our right lay the Sea of Galilee, brilliantly blue. To our left were the ruins of a second or third century synagogue, probably built on the very site where Jesus spoke the words we heard in our text for the day. Below were the ruins of multiple homes, one of which was thought to be Peter's house. Despite the ruins, the setting was tranquil and exquisite.

Reflecting on this text, in this setting, I wondered what it must have been like in those days to wake up on Saturday and go to the synagogue. Synagogue as usual. Get up, brush your teeth, put on your best clothes, sit down for a moment, have a cup of coffee, look at your wife, and ask the question. "Well, shall we go or shall we not? We're supposed to, of course. But it sure would be nice to read the Saturday morning scroll instead of going there."

But, dutifully, they went and as usual there were the scribes sitting down, pouring over the scrolls of the day. The thought and the feeling was basically, "Ho-hum." No impression. Another Sabbath come and gone, and not much had happened.

And then, one Sabbath, everything was radically turned around. Things changed. Jesus came on the scene. That Sabbath he spoke. We are told that he taught not as the scribes taught, but he taught with authority. We are told it made an impression on the people. Something changed in their lives. Something happened.

Then, as if to prove his point, Mark trots out a man who is filled with an evil spirit. The second part of our text portrays exactly what the people had realized. Jesus teaches with authority.

Over in the corner of the tabernacle or near the tabernacle in the synagogue, all of a sudden, a man, who is filled with demons, convulses as these demons speak through him and acknowledge who Jesus is. In doing so they say Jesus' name and try to get power over him.

Jesus tells them, "Be quiet. Get out of the man." The man convulses again and the demons leave. Again the people are astounded. By what authority does this man teach? Even the demons obey him. The news spreads through the countryside. Something has happened.

Sunday morning. Augustana College. Time to get up, hit the shower. Women trotting down the hall with little buckets filled with all sorts of things. The routine is established firmly there, never a change or a deviation. Everybody has her own stuff and does her own thing.

Guys, on the other hand, operate differently. In the bathroom: "Can I borrow your soap? I forgot mine." "You bet. Say, do you need a toothbrush?" "No, that's OK." "Anybody have a towel?"

Sunday morning. We get out of bed and head for the shower. Oh no, one of the kids got there first. "Hurry up!" we call, and go to the kitchen to make some coffee. Over a cup, we glance at the paper until the shower is free.

"Can you make breakfast while I'm getting ready?" Family fed in shifts, not much talking. "Do we have to go?" "Yes, get your coat on!" Soon the family is in the car on the way to church, each one quietly thinking his or her own thoughts.

Church is about to start. We hurry to find a seat. It is Sunday morning as usual. We each come, oftentimes more out of habit than anything else, with our own little mind-set. We sing the songs, pray the prayers, and hear the sermons, but have we allowed ourselves to be touched? Are our lives changed? Has anything happened to us?

Has the word impacted our lives? Has it changed who we are and the perspectives we have?

Probably, we do not come looking for change. After all, change is frightening and can be painful. We like things the way they are. We work hard to carve out a life that is comfortable, safe, and routine. We try to achieve a life where we have our ego satisfied, where we receive some kind of praise in the eyes of our colleagues, where we get some kind of glory.

We try to find some meaning in our life and in our existence. We do not like to be shaken and rattled. We do not like to be confronted. We do not like to hear the truth when the truth hurts and requires change. We easily turn ourselves off to the word read from the texts, to the prayers prayed by us all, to the words of the hymns we all sing. We fear it might make us live a life different from the life we are living.

The majority of college students across the country say their number one goal is to make money in order to have a new car and a new house and all the other materialistic things we often seek. Our Gospel calls that into question, and we do not like hearing it.

Looking at our world, we see injustice, brokenness, and gross inequity. If we actually pay attention, it might require some kind of sacrifice, a whole new direction in our lives, a life given to mission, a life given to service, a life given to self-sacrifice. It scares us. We try to shut it out.

But something happened that Sabbath at the synagogue. The word of Jesus, spoken with authority, cuts through all of that. Our text says it made an impression on them, different from listening to the scribes. The word had power. It was a word that was able to confront the reality of evil, personified in the demons that possessed the man.

Most of us do not even believe in demons, let alone that Jesus can cast them out. Yet, how naïve can we be about the reality of evil and brokenness in our world.

I was at Yad Vashem in Jerusalem—the memorial to the holocaust. I walked through and looked at picture after picture and read word after word about how millions of people had suffered and were slaughtered like a herd of animals. I thought to myself, How can we possibly ever be naïve about the reality of evil in this world.

We think too small in terms of our God and far too small in terms of the power and the reality of evil. It infects our lives and touches us on a global scale, and it does battle with us on a personal scale. "We battle not against flesh and blood, but against powers and principalities," and that is true.

We comfortably pretend life is simply as we see it, and we get lost in the day-to-day rhythms of life. We set little achievable goals that focus around ourselves, goals we can check off, a checklist of life. We pretend that the status quo is just fine. We are comfortable.

And yet, I know that within each of us is a restlessness, a yearning, a drive for a different life. Here is where the Word of God comes to us again. It tells us of a power that is effective, the power of the Word of Jesus Christ.

As the demons were cast out of the man, know that the Word of Jesus Christ in your life is every bit as powerful. It is that same Word that said, "Let there be light," and there was light, creating a force and power beyond anything we can imagine. That word comes to us and says, "My brother, my sister, your sins are forgiven."

We are forgiven, not because of anything we do, not because of the kind of sorrow we can whip up until we finally have enough and, therefore, have earned our forgiveness. It comes to you as grace. It comes to you in love. There's power there. This power can deal with the brokenness in your life. It can transform your life into a vehicle through which that power and authority in Jesus Christ is spread throughout the world.

If he does not use you, whom will he use?

This text challenges each of us to turn away from a life that is shallow, empty, self-centered, and going nowhere, and invites you and me to be agents of that powerful, effective, world-changing, life changing Word coming to us from Jesus Christ.

Reflection

1985 was the year that Mark made the move from serving as campus pastor to Augustana students, faculty, and staff, to becoming vice-president for human relations at the Evangelical Lutheran Good Samaritan Society national campus in Sioux Falls.

He did so with sadness at leaving, because he loved his work at

Augustana, especially with the students. But part of him had longed to work for the Society for a very long time, ever since he had hitch-hiked to Colorado when he was 17 to work as a nursing assistant for the Good Samaritan facility at Greeley. His grandfather's role in creating the Society and his love for older people also drove his passion to work with "Good Sam." His dream was realized and finalized as he moved up to lead the Society as President and CEO in 1989.

Mark was a person who loved each day and did not pine for some future fantasy, but he also embraced change. He loved a new challenge and the variety it would add to life. His ability to see the big picture and quickly figure out how an organization worked enabled him to move into a different line of work easily.

I knew in my heart, when he went to work for the Good Samaritan Society, that I would lose part of him. Since his grandfather had founded the society, and his uncles and father had worked for Good Sam, he felt personally obligated to do a great job. He also loved the work, and the job was so big it was never done. Consequently, he spent over 200 days a year on an airplane, visiting facilities, speaking at anniversaries, and going to board meetings.

I was happy for Mark because he loved his work so much, and it was his dream job. Not many of us get to have our dream job, but he did. However, it was not easy to lose so much of our time together. The distance took a toll on our relationship.

I was never a person who embraced change or longed to experience all the differences the world could provide me. Instead, I was shy as a child, and, for most of my early adulthood, often felt inadequate in my roles as mother, professor, coach, and wife. I longed for routine and stability!

Earlier in my life, going through college days and early on in parenting, I often questioned the reality of God. Our dear friends from St. Olaf, Lois and Chuck Halberg, had a beautiful boy, Scott, who was diagnosed with cancer and died when he was just two. I could not understand a God who would allow that to happen.

Fear and doubt haunted me. What if something happens to one of our kids? And some things did, but not death. Rachel was diagnosed with Type One diabetes when she was six and had many close calls from low blood sugar. Living with childhood diabetes was not easy for Rachel (or for her parents), but she never complained and took care of herself well. Mike came close to falling off the side of a mountain and, when he worked construction one summer, was a few seconds away from being electrocuted.

Sarah contracted a severe upper respiratory infection, perhaps MRS, when we lived in International Falls. She was just four weeks old, and Mark was out of town for the weekend. The other kids were sick as well, but she was really struggling, and started turning blue.

Taking her outside in the thirty below weather seemed to help her breathing as we headed to the hospital. Terrified that she would not make it through the night, I was paralyzed with fear and dread.

I know I prayed. But it was a prayer of desperation. Please, God, please. And God did answer.

Was I worthy? Absolutely not. Do I wonder if she would have gotten better even if I had not prayed? Yes, those thoughts creep in. But I want to believe there is a God who listens, want to believe that this God cares, want to believe that this listening, caring God intervened and saved my baby. And so, in my better moments, the faith/doubt balance shifts to faith.

The power that Jesus wielded in the text woke the people up. It made them aware of themselves and their relationship to God, to worship and to prayer. It changed some of them.

One of the most incredible life changes I know about on a personal level was made by Jane Erdenberger, the wife of Mark's cousin Mark Hoeger of Omaha. Jane was a partner in a prestigious law firm in Omaha—Kutak Rock. She helped finalize big deals with big companies, often traveling to New York and London.

But after time, Jane thought about her job and what she was accomplishing. She was making money, but it seemed devoid of real purpose and meaning. Quietly she started taking night classes at the university to get her teacher's certificate.

After a few years, she finished and was certified to teach high school English and political science. She asked to be placed in the toughest inner-city school in Omaha. Talk about change! Sometimes she wondered why she had done it. But she poured herself, her time and her love into teaching, and more importantly, into her students.

Today she would tell you her life is full of meaning, and she would not change a thing. Still not a cakewalk, but she does have the respect and affection of the students and other teachers in the school, and she has made a huge difference in the lives of many.

Every day every one of us has a chance to make a difference. It might be a major life change, such as Mark's Aunt Agnes giving her life to the mission fields of New Guinea for thirty years or Sarah's college friends taking their small children and paying their own way to volunteer at a medical facility in Kijabe, Kenya, for two years.

Or it may mean being committed parents by loving unconditionally and teaching our children about God, faith and doing the right thing, as I observe Mike and Kelly and Rachel doing while interacting with their children. Sarah's presence and joyful faith also make a difference in the lives of her nieces and nephews.

We all have demons that need to be cast out. The Good News is that God wants to do that for us. God wants us to use our lives, which are being daily resurrected, in loving service of each other.

Aunt Sarah embracing her niece, Sarah

When Even Our Hearts Condemn Us

Hear these words of John from his first letter, Chapter 3: *By this we shall know that we are of the truth, and reassure our hearts before Him, whenever our hearts condemn us, for God is greater than our hearts, and He knows everything.* I John 3:19-20, RSV

While I was sitting in my little office at a camp one summer, a young student came in and started to visit. She spilled out a tale of her own life that was filled with tragedy and brokenness. Toward the end, she stopped, and I saw her lips start to quiver just a little, and tears squeezed out of her eyes and trickled down her cheeks, and she said these words, carefully chosen, I know, "Pastor, I feel so damned guilty."

So guilty. We all understand that. A recent survey among churchwomen in this country shows that the number one burden they live with is the burden of, if you can believe it, guilt. Tucked away is that shadow. Hovering over is that cloud. When we say the word guilt, all kinds of images from the Bible flood my mind.

I think of David, sitting proudly on his throne thinking that he had concealed his illicit relationship with Bathsheba. And the prophet Nathan, standing before him, looking him full in the face and telling him about a rich man who had stolen a little sheep from another. David, in anger, says, "that man must be punished." And then Nathan looks at him, his finger pointing right at him, and says,

"King David, thou art the man." There isn't a one of us who hasn't felt that "thou art the man," or, "thou art the woman."

Other images from the Bible flood my mind. I think of the woman, the prostitute, in shame, but then in hope and repentance, coming before Jesus, washing his feet with her tears, wiping them with her hair.

Or I think of Psalm 32, second and third verses, where the psalmist says, *"when I did not confess my sin I was in anguish all the night long. Thy hand was heavy upon me."* Images of guilt and struggle. I think of Saint Paul saying, *"O wretched man that I am. Who will deliver me from this body of guilt? The good that I would do that I do not and the evil that I would not, that I do."*

Can we not all relate and understand? Or I think of Martin Luther, who struggled with this and who said, *"Though my sins are forgiven, this stumbling block continues to return. I cannot live without a sob, without shame, without blushing."*

I think about us. I think that each one of us knows only too well what it is like to not only be, but to feel, guilty. And so, when we hear words like this from our text our ears perk up. *"By this we shall know that we are of the truth, and reassure our hearts before him whenever our hearts condemn us."* We rejoice because we know only too well that sensation of our hearts condemning us, or, in other translations, our conscience condemning us.

What does our text invite us to do? What does it tell us in regard to this most universal of religious questions, the question of guilt? First of all, hear these powerful words. You talk about raw Gospel, laid out right before you. *"God is greater than our hearts, and he knows everything."* There, the writer of this first epistle of John is telling us that even greater than the condemnation of our hearts is the power of God, who knows all, who loves, and who forgives.

This text, first of all, drives us back to him. Our guilt should drive us back to him who is greater than our guilt, push us back to the source of forgiveness, the source of new life! Oh, but we struggle with that. I mean, we struggle. There are roadblocks in the way all over the place. Some of us feel we are just not worthy—my sins are so bad that I really am not worthy of forgiveness.

I have a friend, who has not gained a pound since the first day he was in college. Really. I call his, the pride of no flesh, and some of us have that same kind of pride—pride in our unworthiness. I'm not worthy to be forgiven. I'm too bad.

We need to hear again the simple, raw, straightforward Gospel. How can you possibly say that the passion of our Lord Jesus Christ, who died for you for the forgiveness of your sins, and who was raised so that you might have hope and a new life, how can you possibly say, in the light of that power, he cannot overcome anything that you have done? That his forgiveness cannot touch everywhere?

The Gospel is not a parable here. It is straight out radical power. Know this, brothers and sisters: Worthiness has nothing to do with forgiveness. Worthiness is a gift, absolute, radical, total, and complete. In the name of Jesus Christ, it is for you. Yet some of us can say, "Yes, Pastor, I believe that, but I have trouble forgiving myself. I mean, maybe it is true, but I still have this guilt around me, and I just can't let it go."

The most vivid image I know came from Søren Kierkegaard, who said when we believe like this, it is as though we've spent a year of our life building a beautiful, wonderful house on a gorgeous mountain over-looking the sea with a beautiful view and panorama all around. And then we go and we live in a windowless basement.

If God has forgiven us, then it is our duty and our joy to forgive ourselves, to not let the burden of our sin drag us down, because that becomes the most self-centered kind of life. And we live wallowing in our own guilt, in our own unworthiness, in our own sin, in our own history, looking only at ourselves. All our energy is focused so inward that we have very little left to live as God has invited us to live, that is, trusting in him and loving one another.

Some of us then say, "Oh, yes, I know, but the trouble is this. How can I live in forgiveness when I keep on sinning?" It is as though at the very time that I feel I am asking God for forgiveness, I am making all these fabulous promises. "I'll never do it again. Oh Lord, I promise. My life is going to be different from now on." When we say it, we believe it. And yet a part of us deep down is planning our next sinful episode. If that is the case, if that is our reality, how in the world can I accept the forgiveness of sins from Jesus Christ?

He has not promised we will be perfect in this life, that we will be without sin. He accepts us in our sin. He accepted us in our sin before we even knew about him. That is what his death on the cross is about, and he will accept us in the future in our sin.

"Oh," but you say, "if that's the case, can't I then just go sinning my way into the Kingdom of God. I mean, if his job is to forgive, then I might as well just sin. What's the difference?" You know how the interior war goes on, sinning and asking for forgiveness on and on.

But you've missed the whole point, as the story of the prodigal son shows us so beautifully. Can you imagine that son squirming out of the loving grasp of his father, pushing himself away and going back to the hogs? Of course not. Though there is a struggle there, we pray that God will work on our hearts, and will, in his power, change our hearts and our lives, so we do not live in cheap grace, but we live in the ever present, ever powerful forgiveness of sins.

Because we live in this forgiveness, our text invites us to love one another in word and in deed. Forgiveness frees. It frees us from a preoccupation with self. It frees us for loving and caring and doing deeds of love, of generosity, of kindness. We do not have to waste our energy on ourselves. We can spend that energy on others. That is what it means to obey his command.

And this is his commandment: that we should believe in the

name of his Son, Jesus Christ, and love one another, just as he has commanded us. That is our goal. That is the life we are called to live, a life forgiven by Jesus Christ and set free to love!

"But," you say, "I do not have it within me." That is the most profound thing you've said yet.

But here is something even more profound. By this we know that he abides in us, by the Spirit that he has given us. And there it is. The Holy Spirit of God, the gift given to us in our baptisms and renewed in us through our life, creates a miracle in our life. We are, day by day, slowly fashioned into his likeness. The Spirit changes us so that love is planted, that selfishness is buried, and that we are transformed more and more into the likeness of our forgiving and loving Lord Jesus Christ.

This is the truth. I mean, it really is. The truth is for you, for each of us. We receive and celebrate that gift today, as we come together, shoulder to shoulder, one in our guilt, but even more, one in the forgiveness won by Jesus Christ on the cross, drawn together by the gift of his spirit.

Reflection

When I was young, I remember feeling a cold, numbing fear when I thought about what would happen to me after I died. I have always been a pleaser, and as a youngster, I behaved pretty well most of the time. I had no huge, disgusting sins. But I knew it was not that easy, and that my salvation was not necessarily guaranteed. Deep down I was terrified of going to hell.

Now, well down the road toward the end of my life, I do not worry about it anymore. I know I sin daily and need forgiveness. I know I have made many mistakes and have multiple sins of omission. But the Gospel has penetrated my heart and mind with God's love, which is what I rely on. Now my daily thought and prayer is something like this: forgive my sins, and empower me to love and honor you by loving whomever you place in my life this day.

The funny thing is, I have spent much of my life feeling not OK about myself, feeling lost, feeling like a failure. I think these thoughts and feelings sometimes sent me into months and years of cramming overachievement into the minutes and hours of every day. I made sure my plate was good and full and then added more. Fear of failure is quite a motivating sensation.

I would love to go back and live my life over if I could have the gift of peace and trust that God has placed in my heart in the last 15 years. I cannot help but think I would have been a better wife, a better mother, a better teacher and coach, and a better friend. I did the best I could, but I could not help but feel I was carrying an albatross around my neck on most days.

Coaching was a job I loved, but the hours were not always family friendly. My teams practiced after classes were over, which was usually after 3 p.m. Normally we spent two hours in practice, and then there were individuals who needed extra help, the field that had to be dragged, and reviewing the practice that needed to be done with my assistant coach. I seldom was around when my children came home from school.

One day we had no practice, and I was home when Sarah and Mike came up the driveway after school. I will never forget the scene: "She's home," shouted Mike, and he and Sarah started running and came in the back door at full speed. After hugs, Mike asked the usual question, "What's there to eat?"

Many mothers work and try to balance their time between family and their job—a stressful task we suspect we seldom get right. I would so like to go back and find a way to be home when they came home from school. I feel guilty to this day that I was not there to talk over the day or give them a hug or feed them homemade cookies.

My kids have told me they learned valuable life lessons by being on their own. They very quickly figured out how to do their own laundry, how to fix a tasty snack, and how to solve problems when they fought. They also reminded me that sometimes they got to come along on team trips. California was not a bad destination. Sarah enjoyed that twice and was old enough to enjoy conversations with some of the college players. Mike got in on an NCAA regional tournament trip to Detroit. Rachel was the one who came to Michigan when we played in the final four and cheered as we won a national championship.

I try not to live in the past, either with regret or enthusiasm. Some days I am constantly telling my mind not to go to those stories I want to change. My mind tends to drift away when I am sitting down, and often it happens in church. Such a waste of time and energy. I do pray for God's help so I can keep my mind on the here and now. I suspect God gets tired of hearing that prayer.

Sometimes I daydream about doing something brave and wonderful for someone else, perhaps risking my life. I doubt I would be that brave, given the chance. I listen to reports from Japan about the meltdowns at some of their nuclear energy plants due to the horrific earthquake and following tsunami. Apparently there are people working in those plants where radiation levels are dangerously high, dedicated to doing their job to try to protect others even when their own lives are being threatened. What an amazing example of love.

On my wall hangs a lovely calligraphy of Psalm 131, given to me by my dear friend, Anne Gibbons, which captures the essence of how to live life well:

> *Lord, I have given up my pride*
> *And turned away from arrogance.*
> *I am not concerned with great matters*
> *Or with subjects too difficult for me.*

Instead,
I am content and at peace,
As a child lies quietly in its
Mother's arms,
So my heart is quiet within me.
I will trust in you, Lord, now and
Forever. Psalm 131

Freedom

31 So Jesus said to those who believed in him, "If you obey my teaching, you are really my disciples; 32 you will know the truth, and the truth will set you free." 33 "We are the descendants of Abraham," they answered, "and we have never been anybody's slaves. What do you mean, then, by saying, 'You will be free'?" 34 Jesus said to them, "I am telling you the truth: everyone who sins is a slave of sin. 35 A slave does not belong to a family permanently, but a son belongs there forever. 36 If the Son sets you free, then you will be really free." John 8:31-36

There are moments in our lives, and I have a hunch that each one of us could call them out from our memories, that are seared into our brains like a freeze-frame. Little turning points. Major events. Who knows why they are there? It is as if they were branded smack-dab in the middle of our thinking processes and our memories. One such event happened in the spring of 1976 for me.

Sandy and I were sitting in our living room, quietly chatting about the events of the day. Stereo playing in the background, sunset coming soon promising to be absolutely stunning, soft breeze seducing the drapes over our southwest window into one more dance, warm feelings all around. And then we heard it: the cry. Mike again, no doubt. I often suspected that deep within his genetic pool is a quota for the number of times to cry during the day. And Mike, not quite five, was going to be faithful to that calling, no matter what.

Well, nothing too serious, we thought.

"I'll check on him in a minute," I said. The crying continued, closer to the house. The front door opened, and there he stood. Now it was only the soft cry that told me it was Michael. His face and the front of his torso were covered with blood. It poured out of his nose and mouth. His nose looked like it had been through a meat grinder. I scooped him up—I will never forget the feeling of my hands covered with the warm blood of my son—rushed him to the bathroom and started to clean him up to see what the extent of his injuries were. We called a physician friend who came right over.

An hour later, all the damage had been assessed. He would be OK. A little later that evening, Mike told us what had happened. My son in my arms, we followed the blood spots on the sidewalk to a tree across the street and down the block. High up in the tree, way out on a limb, was a little nest. Mike wanted to see what was in the nest, he said. He described leaning way over and seeing four beautiful, blue eggs. And then, losing his balance on the thin tree branch, he fell twelve feet to the sidewalk, landing on this face.

Another memory was seared into my brain in the fall of 1979. Evening meal enjoyed, dishes done. "Want to go for a bike ride, Dad?" Son Mike.

"You bet! You lead the way."

"Let's go to the island." The island is a place where three streets come together. In the center is a little oasis of grass and trees.

"Want to see how high I can climb that tree?"

"Sure." Had neither of us learned? Mike climbed expertly to near the top.

Then he leaned out on a branch, looked down at me below and with a mischievous look in his eyes, he said, "Hey Dad, catch!"

There is not a one of us who has not fallen, landed smack float on his or her face, and come up bloodied, frightened and hurt. As we experience more of life, we become more and more aware of our brokenness, of our sinfulness, of the power that comes at us from the dark side of our being, of our failures. And each of us stands wounded, enslaved. As we become more and more aware, we realize that this dark side is not only within us, but we see it as part of our world. We become aware of the brokenness, of the injustice, of the wrong penetrating the very core and fabric of all of society, all of life. We see ourselves struggling to come to grips with our faith in the midst of things we sense are wrong. We are a part of injustices that penetrate all of life. And we become slaves to our sin.

Each of us could tell a story of the enslavement we have experienced in our life and in our nation and in our world, and the struggle that we experience on a day to day basis to become free. Think about your story. Then think about the heart of our text, the struggle to proclaim a word of freedom. *"If you continue in my word, you are truly my disciples. And you will know the truth, and the truth will make you free."* Here is the core of resurrection Gospel. *"If the Son makes you free, you will be free indeed."*

No longer need we cower in fear, focusing on our own brokenness, like the battered child who cowers in the corner at the first flash of anger from his or her parent. Through Jesus, the Son of God, we are no longer slaves but children—children who are loved, who are forgiven, who are promised a home forever. You are loved by Almighty God. You are forgiven by him. You are free, free, free! You have been made his children through Jesus.

God's Son has set us free! No, not free for our own license to do as we wish. That is not freedom, but the most perverse kind of slavery. And not free from our depression and quirks of character and warts and hangnails and hemorrhoids, not free from the struggles, pains, sufferings and temptations of life. Not free from hearing the call of our brothers and sisters all over the world, who cry out for justice and freedom and food and a chance for some kind of life, a chance to hear the Good News. God's Son sets us free each day to risk, to live to the fullest, to serve, to spend our life for the sake of all those who suffer under injustice and brutality in this world. Free to serve, to care, to forgive, to be people who bring reconciliation, togetherness, peace. Free in the faith. We can climb the trees of life and each day look into the unknown future, and then, being led by the Gospel, jump into it, with a twinkle in our eyes, a smile on our lips, and a prayer in our hearts. "Hey Dad, catch!"

Reflection

I, too, remember it as though it happened yesterday. Mark and I were having one of our evening conversations about the day when the wailing began, and we really were not too concerned. Until our son came through the front door with a face I did not recognize, full of blood. That moment of horror and fear imprinted itself forever in my mind. The fear began to recede as the doctor examined him and then smiled as he said Mike would be OK. As parents, our nurturing, protective concern for our children hides just under the surface of day-to-day parenting. Being a grandparent is in some ways worse. We know too much about all the black holes in our world and how easily bad things can happen to innocent children.

The freedom we think we have in our country and in our world is a tenuous one. Although we can plan our lives and set goals, things happen. My father's death at an early age turned my world upside down and changed it forever. Not long afterwards, my brother, who was serving in the Navy on the island of Guam, collided with a gravel truck while riding his motorcycle and was killed. It took three weeks before we received his body and had the funeral. His death when I was 17 added to my anxiety about the fragility of life.

Freedom from fear is at the heart of this sermon, and that is precisely what I did not have for much of my life. I never knew when the next shoe would fall, when the next smothering cycle of depression would hit, when I might not be well-enough prepared for a speech, a lesson, a practice, a problem. I never knew when I would forget to do some urgent task or something might happen to one of the children. I never dreamed that my strong, vibrant, full of life husband would be wheeled into his hospital room by his brother and tell me, "I have cancer, and I'm not going to beat it."

In between my fits of fear and whenever I could get out from underneath what felt like a fifty-pound weight on my shoulders, I lived and loved life. I whipped up Swedish pancakes for my family for breakfast, swam and took saunas with them at Rainy Lake, traveled all over with my teams, including two self-funded trips to Hawaii, and cherished many satisfying friendships. I had a husband who encouraged me in all my undertakings, including going back to school to get a master's degree and a doctorate. And when he was the President and CEO of the Good Samaritan Society, he would say, "I'm just the coach's husband"—and mean it.

I believe Mark was talking about living our lives trusting that God will be present for us always. No one gets out of this life without observing and experiencing bad things. None of us is perfect. In his last weeks and days, Mark talked about how at peace he felt facing his own death. "I have to say, I wonder if I have been given a gift. I mean, I'm surely not in denial. If anyone has accepted the reality of their death much sooner than normal, it is I." And he would smile.

"The gift of faith. Maybe I'm not angry because I'm so hopeful for life beyond this life. I will be honest; I know my life is in the hands of the Lord. I cannot fantasize anything better than that."

I know what he was talking about because when he died he passed that gift along to me, like a runner passing off a baton. Although I intensely grieved his absence for about five years, and being alone is not easy, I have felt fully supported by the gift of trust, of peace. What an astonishing gift—as if an invisible, outstretched hand supports and blesses every day. Let me give an example.

Late in the afternoon on a gray, depressing fall day, I parked my dirty old campaign van in the parking lot by the bank in Tea and crossed the street to start "doing doors" for my inaugural campaign in 2006. The first door was always the hardest. I often wondered what in the world I was doing out there. I walked hesitatingly to the door, located on the side of the little home.

Suddenly, the door swung open and a man stepped out, introduced himself as Jeff, saying loudly, "Sandy, you're going to win!"

I could only grin. That was quite an opening. We chatted a little while, and then he asked me, "Say, do you need any money?"

I was truly a novice then, so I hemmed and hawed and said, "No, I'm OK."

"Wait here." When Jeff came back, he had a $100 bill in his outstretched hand. "Don't tell my wife." His eyes twinkled. "Do you remember the night in the hospital when your husband was dying?"

"Yes," I said. How could I forget?!

"Well, remember how you lost the diamond ear rings your husband had given you for your birthday, and how upset you were?"

"Yes," I said, that memory tucked deeply in my heart.

"Well," he responded, "That cleaning lady who found those ear rings and gave them to you is my wife."

Suddenly the dreary afternoon became a gift, dispelling fear, and I knew the visit had not been just with Jeff.

Death Defeated

17 Some time later the widow's son got sick; he got worse and worse, and finally he died. 18 She said to Elijah, "Man of God, why did you do this to me? Did you come here to remind God of my sins and so cause my son's death?" 19 "Give the boy to me," Elijah said. He took the boy from her arms, carried him upstairs to the room where he was staying, and laid him on the bed. 20 Then he prayed aloud, "O Lord my God, why have you done such a terrible thing to this widow? She has been kind enough to take care of me, and now you kill her son!" 21 Then Elijah stretched himself out on the boy three times and prayed, "O Lord my God, restore this child to life!" 22 The Lord answered Elijah's prayer; the child started breathing again and revived. 23 Elijah took the boy back downstairs to his mother and said to her, "Look, your son is alive!" 24 She answered, "Now I know that you are a man of God and that the Lord really speaks through you!" I Kings 17:17-24

Death had ravaged her home and her life before. She remembered how lonely she had become when death stole her husband, how hard it had been to live on charity. But at least she had her son, someone to love, someone to care for, a reason to live. They made out all right for a while, this widow from Zarephath and her little son. But death stalked them again, hunted them down and had them cornered during the drought. She remembered how she had gone out to gather some firewood to prepare her last bit of food. They might die, but at least they would die together. There was a strange bit of comfort in that.

And then that crazy old man Elijah came into her life. Man of God, he called himself. "Don't worry about food," he said. "God will take care of you." He moved into the little room upstairs. It was good, she remembered. There was food for them each day. And it was nice to have a man around the house again. A few of the old gossips whispered when she passed them on the street. But she did not mind.

And then death came again, slowly squeezing the life from her little boy. She had prayed and prayed, hoped and hoped. After all, that man of God was living in her house. But her son got worse and finally died. As she held the still-warm body of her dead son in her arms, her world fell apart. She was overwhelmed with a sense of guilt from her past. The years of lonely, meaningless life ahead of her surrounded her like a shroud.

She looked at Elijah. "Is God punishing me?" She thought. *"Man of God, why did you do this to me? Did you come here to remind God of my sins and so cause my son's death?"*

"Give the boy to me," Elijah said. He took the boy from her arms and she looked at him carrying her son up the stairs to his room. The next words she heard were Elijah's: *"Look, your son is alive!"*

Prayer answered. New life for her son and for her. Death defeated. Or was it?

"The last enemy to be defeated will be death," St. Paul tells us. And he is right. Death is an enemy. At times it masquerades as a friend. When it takes an old person who has suffered long, we say, "My wasn't it a blessing." But do not be deceived. Paul was right. Death is our enemy. For it haunts us, confronts us with our own finiteness, capriciously reaches into our community and snatches one whom we love from our midst.

After the death of his wife, William Armstrong wrote these

words: "How do you tell your children their mother has died? I cannot tell them separately. They must all come down together. Each day Kip saves a little love, a little energy, a few thank yous to begin the next day. Today Kip will save the broken pieces of his heart. David is a year and a half younger than Kip. He will be seven in six more weeks; he rides harder and sleeps longer. David puts all his love, all his energy, all this thank yous into each day. Today his heart will break, and there will be no pieces big enough to save.

"Mary, who the boys fondly call 'Sis,' will be the last to waken. She went with Mommy yesterday to get the invitations for her birthday party. She will be five in seven more days.

"They are coming down the stairs, innocently laughing and racing. They are almost at my door..."

The enemy has struck again. And he seldom comes alone. He brings with him guilt, hopelessness, doubt. The question of the widow in Zarephath is one that is asked in a thousand different ways, but the variations are always on the same theme: "Did you come here to remind God of my sins and so cause my son's death?"

In the face of that last enemy, where can we turn? To whom can we go? There is something incomplete about the story of the widow's son being restored to life. It is a beautiful story, to be sure. It could almost end with "...and they lived happily ever after." But, of course, they didn't. In that instance death took it on the chin, but it was not defeated. The widow eventually died, and her son died. In the face of these deaths, this beautiful little story drives us beyond itself. For death still confronts us, and it often brings guilt and despair.

This story drives us beyond the Old Testament to the New Testament, to our question of where to turn in the face of death. *"Did you come here to remind God of my sins and so cause my son's death?"* To the questions that we struggle with, which reminds us of the widow's question to Elijah, the surprising answer comes to us from God himself.

The Gospel of John says it so well: *"For God loved the world so much that he gave his only Son, so that everyone who believes in him may not die but have eternal life. For God did not send his Son into the world to be its judge, but to be its savior,"* (John 3:16-17). Here is the promise of forgiveness, here is the promise of life: in the death and resurrection of Jesus we have been offered the gift of life beyond this life. Hope is restored. We rest in the trust that God will take us all home to be with him.

Reflection

When Mark was diagnosed with terminal cancer, although he accepted the facts, he still hoped and prayed for life, as much life here on earth as possible. We both did. And that is all any of us have—a measured amount of time here on earth. As Mark reminded us, none of us is going to get out of this life alive. Death waits for all of us. One of the comments Mark made was, "At least I don't have to worry about getting Alzheimer's."

During the months Mark was dying, he used to say he had a "church without walls." Many friends came to visit him, to minister to him, and to say goodbye. He usually ended up ministering to them, helping them accept death as a part of life, and giving them comfort—and, most likely, giving them something to laugh about.

Yet, it does still feel like death has the upper hand. For instance: My dear friend, Randy Kouri, a kind and good man who loved his family, just died. In Japan, death reigned, claiming tens of thousands of lives in the latest earthquake and tsunami. More recently, in Norway dozens of young people were gunned down in a senseless slaughter by a deranged right-wing bigot.

My daughter, Sarah, called me one day sobbing. She is a psychologist at Children's Hospital in St. Paul and was new at her job.

She had been caring for a three-year-old little girl with cute curls and an adorable smile who had cancer. And died. She went to the wake to support the family and saw the child lying motionless in her little coffin with a favorite teddy bear snuggled under her arm. "She looked like any minute she would open her eyes and smile at us!" wailed Sarah.

Why? Why? Why?! But wherever death is kept at bay, and a life is pulled back from the abyss, be it a miraculous recovery from cancer, or a man's heart beat being restored after a heart attack, or a child saved from drowning, I cheer. I embrace God's promises to take us home. But here on earth we experience finality, grief, despair, and suffering surrounding a death. It also seems extremely capricious and unjust. I know Job got chewed out by God (*"Where were you when I laid the foundation of the earth?"*) when he questioned why everything in his life had fallen apart. I'm just saying. There it is.

Death struck fear into my heart at an early age. First it was my neighbor, whose wife ran out of the house screaming, "No. No," after he had a heart attack and died. Then it was Linda Macki's grandmother, who had a heart attack while we were staying with her in their cabin by the lake. By the time the ambulance arrived, she had soiled her bed and was going downhill fast. The EMTs loaded her up in the back, and then sat up front, while Linda and I held Grandma's hands as her life slipped away on the 30-mile trip to the hospital. I was 11.

The worst, of course, when I was young was my own father and best friend dying of a heart attack at age 53. Three and a half years later came the word of my brother's death. We had become friends before he died, and I missed him terribly.

Mark's illness and death was, of course, the biggest hit of all. He was just 54 when he died, and my mother, who was 95, said through her tears, "I never wanted this to happen to you." But the comment Mark made to my mother, Phoebe, when he was dying was even more poignant, "Phoebe, you wanted me to preach at your funeral, and I'm afraid I'm not going to be here to do that." Phoebe died two years after Mark, at 96.

It's painful. It's not fair. And it's random. After all these years, let me tell you what I think. Though it feels like our world has fallen apart and grief will never end when death descends on us, God helps us, often through the ministry of others.

After my father died, I remember my mom's friend Pat, who would drive by my childhood home after 10:30 p.m. about twice a week and come in for a cup of tea if the light was on, which it usually was. That helped my mother immensely. The outpouring of love both before and after Mark died carried me like the crest of a wave through the months following his death. Now I can be part of that ministry to others, trying to remember, from time to time, to visit those who have lost a loved one.

Remembering to be grateful for what I had is also helpful. I had a great marriage to a great guy. I have the family I longed for, children to love and hold, and now, grandchildren. I am blessed. I had loving parents, who gave me my life values and faith. I remember with joy sitting in my father's lap and listening to the St. Olaf Choir. I remember my mother's unique sense of humor and pride in being my mother. I remember Mark's arm around me whether at home or church, and the warmth of his body next to mine in bed. More than memories, these are a part of the fabric of my life.

Mark's mother, Laura, will soon be 92. I am traveling to Florida to spend time with her and help her celebrate her birthday. She is full of joy and excitement for living and is fit and sharp mentally. She enjoys every minute we spend together, as she does with her other children and their families. But she speaks easily about going home to be with the Lord and her dear husband and son. She longs for it. For now, that is how we defeat death.

The Rich Man

17 As Jesus was starting on his way again, a man ran up, knelt before him, and asked him, "Good Teacher, what must I do to receive eternal life?" 18 "Why do you call me good?" Jesus asked him. "No one is good except God alone. 19 You know the commandments: 'Do not commit murder; do not commit adultery; do not steal; do not accuse anyone falsely; do not cheat; respect your father and your mother.'" 20 "Teacher," the man said, "ever since I was young, I have obeyed all these commandments." 21 Jesus looked straight at him with love and said, "You need only one thing. Go and sell all you have and give the money to the poor, and you will have riches in heaven; then come and follow me." 22 When the man heard this, gloom spread over his face, and he went away sad, because he was very rich. 23 Jesus looked around at his disciples and said to them, "How hard it will be for rich people to enter the Kingdom of God!" 24 The disciples were shocked at these words, but Jesus went on to say, "My children, how hard it is to enter the Kingdom of God! 25 It is much harder for a rich person to enter the Kingdom of God than for a camel to go through the eye of a needle." 26 At this the disciples were completely amazed and asked one another, "Who, then, can be saved?" 27 Jesus looked straight at them and answered, "This is impossible for human beings but not for God; everything is possible for God." Mark 10:17-27

I have often wondered what drove that particular man to run up to Jesus and ask that question. Why in the world would he ever be concerned about something like that? After all, we're told that this man was wealthy—a rich man. That is something—to wake up in the morning and know you never have to worry about anything financial. Your tuition is not due; it has already been paid. For four years! And a few thousand extra are thrown in just in case you need some more meal tickets.

You have no worries about a thing. When you want to go to a movie, instead of taking the bus, you just hop into your Corvette and off you go. You don't have to worry about the cost of gas, because you're set. You've got it.

Once there was a rich man. Phenomenally rich. And not only was he wealthy, but he was well respected in his community. He did not get his money from shady dealings. When he walked down the street, people would say to him, "Well, hello. How are you? It's good to see you. Come and have some coffee. I want to visit with you." He was liked and respected. I wonder why he came to Jesus and asked him, "Sir, what must I do to have eternal life?" I've often wondered.

Different from most of us, he was not even plagued with a guilty conscience. Now I suspect not one of us here does not know what a guilty conscience is all about. We have all had that struggle.

Yet, when Jesus said to him, "All you have to do—do you know the commandments? Obey them," he answered, "But sir, I have obeyed these commandments since my youth."

And yet something was not right. He had wealth and possessions. He was well respected and admired in his community. He went to sleep at night with a clear conscience. He did his best to keep the commandments perfectly. Yet, something was wrong inside. He had that haunting, nagging feeling that surely there is more to life than this. He did not laugh from his stomach. He was hollow. Maybe he was about my age, forty—mid-life crisis time. Who knows? But all he knew was that somehow he was all bound up, tied up. He was not free. Something was horribly wrong with his life.

He had heard the rumor about a teacher named Jesus. Maybe he would have the answer. When he found Jesus, he posed this question, "What do I have to do to inherit eternal life?" It finally hit him. That was the issue—the ultimate issue of his life.

So it is with us. What must we do to have eternal life? Lest you think this is a story about someone different from you because you certainly are not rich, let me tell you straight out, my friends, you're loaded! You just have to take a look at yourself from the point of view of most of the world to know how rich you really are!

You are rich because you have enough money to attend Augustana. Rich because you have food, and you have clothes, and you have so many clothes you have to decide what to wear on a given day. You are rich! You have material possessions like most of the world would kill for!

Oh, we are loaded. But riches and wealth has to do with more than things or possessions. A wealthy person is a person who has options and opportunities. How wealthy you are! You have the whole world in front of you. It is phenomenal the choices and the options that you and I have, and how rich we are.

Our text does not give the man's name. "There was a man" is all it says. And the Gospel writer does that for a purpose. He does it because he wants us to see that this text is for every person, every man and every woman. It speaks to us all.

"What must we do to gain eternal life?" Have you wondered that yourself? Has that been a question that you have struggled with? Has it been a part of your life, in one way or another? Have you found dissatisfaction with things, with stuff, with position, even with nice, warm, fuzzy feelings? Have you ever sensed that surely there's got to be more? In the words of that old song, "Is that all there is? Then break out the booze and have a ball, 'cause that's all there is."

But, in hope, the rich man went up to Jesus and asked. What did Jesus say? Strange, he said, "Have you kept all the commandments?" This coming from a man of love who discounted people who claimed their salvation by the commandments. He listed them off, a typical rabbi response to a typical question often asked of a rabbi. The man said, "Yes, from my youth."

Then our Gospel says this, and it is beautiful; *"Jesus looked straight at him with love and said, 'Only one thing you lack. Sell everything you have, give it to the poor, and you will have the kingdom of God. Then come and follow me.'"* There it was before him, straight out. Nothing ambiguous. No questions. The offer, given by the Son of God.

Wouldn't you snap it up? Tell me, would you? Thank about it for a minute. If you knew that all you had to do was sell all that you have, give it away to the poor, and find a way to follow the Lord, and you would know beyond the shadow of a doubt that eternal life would be guaranteed for you. Wouldn't you do it right now? Or are we more like that rich man?

"When he heard this, he was shocked," we are told, *"and went away grieving, for he had many possessions."* To whom much has been given, much is required. How about you?

If the story ended here, it would be, to my way of thinking, the most tragic, hopeless story in the whole Bible, and it would fill me with absolute, total despair and hopelessness. I would feel tied up, bound.

So were the disciples, suddenly. They, too, saw what was happening, and they said to him, "Lord, what's going on?" Jesus explained, *"How hard it will be for those who have wealth to enter the kingdom of God. It is easier for a camel to go through the eye of a needle than for someone who is rich to enter the kingdom of God."* In other words, it is literally impossible.

The disciples then ask the question we would ask, *"Who then can be saved?"* That is the question. Jesus says it straight; he says, *"For mortals it is impossible."* Absolutely impossible. He seems to contradict what he said before. Even if you did sell all that you have and give it to the poor, that would not be enough. It would free you up from those things that are binding you, but even to do that would be a miracle, an absolute miracle.

Then comes the most beautiful little Gospel word in all of Mark: *"But,"* says Jesus, *"for God, all things are possible."* Listen. Listen. Listen to the answer to our ultimate question—the question of our eternal life, of our salvation. Know that it is a work of God, a gift from God, from beginning to end. Absolutely, literally, a miracle.

Because of that gift of God, Jesus Christ came to this earth, died and was raised again so that we have the possibility of eternal life. Through the gift of God, Jesus' Spirit comes to us. Through the gift of baptism, having done nothing to deserve it, we receive a pure gift of God, because he loves us.

Through his Holy Spirit, we have the gift of faith. We cannot just decide one day to have faith. When we feel faith growing in our hearts and our lives, it is the Spirit of God working within us that allows that faith to deepen and be nurtured. This gift of faith is a pure gift from God, who loved us enough to die for us, and who loves us with an everlasting love.

Read Romans, chapter three, and hear it again from St. Paul: *"It is not a work, lest anyone should boast, but purely God's gift of grace."* That is Gospel. The Good News. I do not have to worry about salvation, about whether I have done enough or believed enough. Salvation, from now through eternity, is all gift, flowing from God's love and mercy to us, his people.

In whose hands would you rather have your salvation than in God's hands? Do you want it in your own hands? I surely don't. But God loves us with an eternal love, and gives us an eternal promise: *"I go to prepare a place for you."* And what does God require of you? To love mercy and do justice and walk humbly with God? To love God with all your heart and your neighbor as yourself? To simply offer God your heart, with a will to love?

These are all good things to do, but the answer is nothing. Nothing is required. God has done it all for us. The price has been paid in full. We can do nothing to procure our own salvation. But what would you do for a person who has bailed you out of a lifetime sentence in prison? How would you respond to someone who laid down his life so you could live? How could you thank someone, who took all the bad and wrong things you have ever said or done in your life, and forgave them and wiped the slate clean?

I am convinced that we have only half the story told in the Gospel of Mark. I am convinced that the look of love did something to that wealthy man. I am convinced that, somewhere along the line, he found the courage, the miracle we're talking about, to free himself from the slavery of all his possessions and his stuff, and found the courage to follow Jesus in his own way.

I pray that each of us will find the courage to live our lives as the saved, loved, forgiven, and freed people in Jesus Christ that we are. I pray that we will decide again for Jesus, day after day, and that, in the freedom of that gift of the Gospel, we will spend ourselves in gratitude to our Lord. For God has provided us with every good gift, and we are wealthy, indeed.

Reflection

This story, told in the Gospels of Matthew and Mark, was a favorite for Mark and me. Who has not worried at some point in time about eternal life and whether or not the gate would be open for us? Although Jesus hits the rich man at his most vulnerable point—his riches—he invites him to come and follow him, to be with him. It is a picture of priorities, and how we often order our priorities. We would rather not have to do without our stuff and our comforts, even if it means losing out on a relationship with Jesus.

But even when we make bad choices, and turn our backs on Jesus in lieu of hanging onto our possessions, Jesus still points to his father, our God, who can still grant us eternal life with him. There is such hope in this story and such reality of our weaknesses and the power of God.

Mark was never a rich man in the real sense of the word. When compared to the rest of the world, probably most Americans are rich. But in terms of having real wealth and living a lifestyle of one who has wealth, Mark was not in that category. He grew up in a home of six children, and his father was a Lutheran minister. His mother stayed at home with the children. Often the money would run out before the end of the month.

Mark put himself through college and the seminary, paying off school debts well into his forties. Since he was also a Lutheran minister, we, like his parents, had no money left over at the end of the month to put into savings or retirement funds.

As a result, when they were in high school, all of our children were encouraged to get a job, especially in the summer, to help out with their expenses. Mike worked at Macy's during the school year and a construction company during the summer, and Sarah worked at a car wash and Hy-Vee. Rachel worked at a fast-food place as her first job, but then took on a job I wasn't sure she would stick with: serving as a certified nursing assistant at a Good Samaritan facility. But she found her niche and loved it. I will never forget her walking up the driveway sobbing one night after one of her favorite residents had died during her shift. Rachel has a loving heart for people, especially the elderly, as her father did.

As my mother, Phoebe, grew old, Rachel often spent time with her, smoothing lotion into her arms and legs. Rachel's love was evident as she cared for my mother's dry, fragile skin and also as she touched and embraced her.

Phoebe and Rachel

Growing up, I was not rich either. My father was the superintendent of schools, and my mother stayed at home. Both had grown up poor and had gone through the Great Depression, so they were very frugal with their money. We were the last ones on the block to buy a TV, when I was in fifth grade. But I never sensed financial distress.

When Mark and I lived in Richmond, Virginia, for a year following his seminary years, and he was again going to school, we were indeed poor. I typed papers to earn a little money, and Mark allowed the A. H. Robins drug company to test drugs on his body to see if they were safe for use in order to earn some extra cash. I baked not-for-consumption cookies to decorate our little Christmas tree, which had no lights. And yet, we did not feel poor.

Later, three years before Mark became ill, we visited Nepal and hiked into the foothills of the Himalayan Mountains, where we met women carrying water on their heads from a great distance, women who always smiled and said, "Namaste," peace. Our young guide stopped at a cave on the side of a mountain, and as we sat at a small table, a man came out with tea and omelets. He had a huge smile on his face. Poor they were in material goods, but not poor in spirit.

Mark had a keen aesthetic sense. He used to comment on scenes in nature or works of art at a gallery, "What a feast for the eyes." So much in my world is a feast for the eyes—my magenta and cream tiger lilies blossoming and welcoming me to a new day, a stunning sunset over Rainy Lake, the ecstasy of my granddaughter

Catherine, as she dances outside to take a ride in my golf cart. I have eyes to see. I am blessed. I am rich, indeed.

These little stories illustrate a well-known truth. Riches do not produce happiness, nor does a lack of material goods necessarily cause unhappiness. In the text, Jesus sensed that the rich man was not at peace and was still seeking meaning in life. Jesus' invitation to him to get rid of his stuff and follow Jesus gave him a clear direction to peace.

At the same time, Jesus pointed out that anyone, who has more than they need for survival, is in danger of heading in the wrong direction in life and may not find redemption and eternal life. But the word Mark and I hung onto was that God can do anything, including redeeming us, all of us, even when we have too much or love our stuff more than God or more than other people in our lives.

My dear friend Ann Eichinger is a retired librarian and lives an unencumbered lifestyle, including driving an old car. Last year she drove back and forth between Pierre, South Dakota, and Sioux Falls every week, volunteering her time for her friend, Scott Heidepriem, as he ran for governor, and taking care of her elderly landlady on the weekends. She completely gave up her life in this way for 16 months, taking no money for her service. Not wealthy, she was rich in love and had heartfelt compassion for others.

One day when Jesus was observing who gave what offering, he pointed out to his disciples that the two pennies dropped into the plate by a widow would be more honored by God than any of the other larger offerings, because she gave all she had.

Money, money, money. A blessing and a curse, depending on how we use it and how we think about it. I am quite sure I never get it right, but I try, and I will keep trying, and I will pray for wisdom and forgiveness, trusting that with God all things are possible.

Dreams

16 Instead, this is what the prophet Joel spoke about: 17 'This is what I will do in the last days, God says: I will pour out my Spirit on everyone. Your sons and daughters will proclaim my message; your young men will see visions, and your old men will have dreams. 18 Yes, even on my servants, both men and women, I will pour out my Spirit in those days, and they will proclaim my message;' Acts 2:16-18

September of 1960. Boe Memorial Chapel, St. Olaf College. Opening convocation. Mark Jerstad, sitting in about the third-to-the-last row on the aisle. David Johnson, the organist, playing from the balcony, let go with one of the most phenomenal pieces of music I have ever heard in my life.

And then, in came the parade. All the professors of St. Olaf College, dressed in full regalia. Big, beautiful academic gowns with stripes on the shoulders and panels running down the front, and behind, hoods—big, beautiful, multi-colored hoods. I did not know what they meant, but I knew they signified importance, because the big shots wore them.

That day an eighteen-year-old young man gave birth to a dream. Someday, he said to himself, I want to walk in that parade. That little dream, born in Boe Memorial Chapel in September of 1960, determined the direction of my life.

Dreams. I wish for you, I pray for you, dreams. Beyond the

kind of dreams that we often harbor: get an education, get married, get a job, have a nice house and a couple of cars in a nice part of town, and live out my life in a nice, day-to-day little secure kind of way.

Not that anything is wrong with that, but there is so much more. I want you to have dreams.

First of all, I invite you to dream big dreams—dreams that are almost phenomenal in your fantasy, dreams that surely can never come true. They are too much, you think. Not little old me!

Dream them. Get rid of those little teeny dreams that are like peas you spill on the floor when eating, and they get over in the corner and are forgotten and just shrivel up and finally are sucked up by the vacuum cleaner. Dream big dreams! Let your fantasy go wild!

Then I invite you to take your dreams, whatever they are, and lay them on the altar. Pass them before our Lord. Let them be dreams that spill forth from the very mind of God, find their way to you, and take up residence.

Finally, it is never enough just to dream. Pray that God's Spirit will empower you to turn those dreams into reality. It can be, for you, dreams much bigger than a hood. After all, what is all that? A pea-size dream. Let big dreams, from God, become flesh in you.

Job said that old men will dream dreams. I am an old man. When I compare myself to you, you are as my children. Let me share my dream of your dreams.

Some day I hope to pick up my *Time* magazine and look inside and see, written in great big, bold print that someone by the name of Sarah sat down and negotiated a nuclear arms treaty whose eventual goal was to rid the world of all nuclear arms.

And I dream of being able to say, "Sandy, remember Sarah who always used to sit right over there in chapel every day?" I have big dreams.

Or I dream of old Johnson, who used to burn his eyes out in

the lab at Gilbert Science and has now discovered the key to the cure for cancer. "Sandy, remember old Johnson? He always used to come dragging in late to chapel, but he'd try to get there whenever he could, books under his arm. Look what he did!" Big dreams.

But dreams cost. They cost Martin Luther King, Jr., his life. They cost Gandhi his whole style of life. They gave to Dag Hammarskjöld a troubled soul and spirit. Nelson Mandela spent most of his adult life in prison.

But look what they have done. A new day of love and acceptance between blacks and whites. A free and democratic India. A stronger United Nations. Freedom in South Africa. Let your dreams be big. Lay them on the altar. Let God's Spirit empower you to discipline yourself and give of yourself in order to turn them into reality. Spend yourself for the sake of others.

Dream, my brothers and sisters, dream. Dream. Dream!

Reflection

This sermon came straight from the heart. If Mark was anything, he was a dreamer. I used to catch him often staring into space with that thousand-yard stare. Something big was always going on when I asked him what he was thinking about.

I was introduced to the absurdness of some of his dreams early on while we were still dating. One night we were out for a walk, one of our favorite pastimes, and all of a sudden under the lamp light Mark pointed to a fancy looking sports car. It was one of those expensive, exotic kinds, perhaps a Lamborghini.

"Someday I am going to own one of those," he stated. I laughed. After all, he was putting himself through college working at the Ford plant. His father was a Lutheran minister barely getting by. Mark was planning on going into the ministry. Perhaps he was thinking of winning the lottery.

Not too long after we were married, while he was a student at Luther Seminary, he bought a used Corvette Sting Ray convertible, 400 hp, for $3500. That was on the income from our summer jobs, teaching swimming. But we had a ball driving and riding in that car all summer. Then he sold it. For $3500.

Many years later he found a DeLorean. A car company in Sioux Falls was trying to get rid of it after John DeLorean had gone to prison and his car company went into bankruptcy. He paid $12,000 for it, and he drove it everywhere for the next ten years, even in the winter.

His favorite use was hauling teen-age kids around, usually stuffing four or five in the two-seater. When Tom Daschle appointed Mike to be a page in the U.S. Senate, Mark drove him to DC in the DeLorean. Mike must have packed light for the year.

Mark had inherited the gene for appreciating unusual and fine cars from his grandfather, who used to own a pair of very expensive horses to pull his carriage. And somehow Mark usually managed to find a price he could afford.

Mark always encouraged his children to dream big, including choosing whatever college they wanted to attend. He didn't want them to feel limited by proximity or money. Somehow, he thought, we could swing it. Mike always dreamed of reaching high and going far, so one fall the family van headed for Boston and Tufts University where Mike began his education. Four years later he went on to Georgetown, where he earned his law degree, and after a few years, he received an MBA from the University of Chicago. The venture capital business fits him well.

Rachel chose Augustana and then finished at Augsburg. Rachel's dream of using her gifts to help others led her from the nursing field to human resources. She later went on to earn a master's degree in human resources from St. Thomas University. Today she uses that degree well as she serves in the human resources department of a world-wide Japanese company.

Sarah chose St. Olaf, where my father had graduated and where Mark and I had met. We were thrilled with the choice, which was entirely hers. Mark would have loved it if Sarah had tried out for one of the choirs, because that was always his dream, but she had poured herself into choirs from 7th grade through her senior year in high school. She wanted to head in a different direction. Her dream was to become a psychologist, which she accomplished, now working as a psychologist at Children's Hospital in St. Paul, Minnesota.

Another one of Mark's dreams was to give away a million dollars in his lifetime. The goal was announced before we were married, and, again, I laughed. Where was that going to come from?!

Later on, after he had become the President and CEO of the Good Samaritan Society, he talked about someday setting up a family foundation to "teach the children about charity, and to bring the family together every year someplace where it was warm in the win-

Letters of Love

ter." I didn't pay much attention to that idea either.

The Good Samaritan Society decided to take out an insurance policy on their CEO, one for the company and one for the family. Mark had a complete physical, which he passed with flying colors. Unfortunately, a colonoscopy was not included, because it may very well have detected the cancer that was growing in his colon. Less than a year later, he was diagnosed with late stage colon cancer.

The doctors predicted he would not survive much longer than a month, because the aggressive cancer was late stage. But Mark went to MD Anderson Cancer Center in Houston, Texas, and was hooked up with a constant infusion chemotherapy treatment. He had a port put in and carried the portable chemotherapy unit.

That treatment, and trying some experimental clinical trials, definitely helped extend Mark's life, but his greatest ally was his attitude. He trusted God with his future and focused on living for as many days as he had. He never felt sorry for himself and often spent visits with old friends laughing about shared stories and reassuring people that he was doing fine.

He also focused on making sure there would be a smooth transition at work, and that ends were tied up at home. About three weeks before he went into the hospital, he planned the creation of the Jerstad Family Foundation with his attorney, Vance Goldammer.

Vance knew sometimes those things took up to a year to finalize with government approval, so he used all the charm he possessed when he got in touch with a woman who was in charge of approving family foundations.

Vance explained Mark's situation and said how much it would mean if he could know the foundation was a done deal before he died. The woman said, "You mean you're asking me to put his application on top of this huge pile I have on my desk?" After Vance indicated that was the case, there was a long pause.

Finally, the woman came back on the line. "It's done," she said, meaning she had taken care of making it an official family foundation. So before Mark died, he knew he would be giving far more than a million dollars to a variety of charitable causes.

Mark could not have left a better gift for the children and me. With joy, we come together at Christmas in front of a fireplace and listen to each other talk with passion about the needs we want to address with grants each year.

Some of the smallest gifts have meant the most and seemed to make the biggest differences. One year the grade school that Rachel, Mike, and Sarah attended suffered the loss of one of the second-grade students, who was murdered by her grandmother's boyfriend. In order to help the students and staff cope with this tragedy, a second-grade teacher had the idea of turning a small room into a peaceful space full of art and hopeful writings, where they could spend some time finding remembrances of the student who died and also find hope and peace for the future. When I heard about it, they just needed $3000 to finish the room before school's end.

It was an easy decision to make. I will never forget when I went to Garfield Elementary School to present the check to the second-grade teacher. The principal and my friend Susan, who taught there came along, too, and we called the teacher out into the hall. I told her that my children, our family foundation board members, had all attended Garfield, and we really wanted to help with this meaningful project through our family foundation. The teacher, the principal, Susan, and I stood in the hallway crying, as the teacher accepted the check and told us how much it meant to her and the students.

Leaving us a family foundation has done just what Mark had hoped, and so much more. Participating in the joy of giving in a personal way, where it makes a difference, gives us great satisfaction and pulls us together as a family.

College scholarships, grants to feeding ministries, support for mental health facilities for the poor, special projects at churches, and educational grants are a few of the many grants we have been able to give out. Mark wanted all proceeds to go to the Good Samaritan Society for the first five years, and during that time we honored his wish, so we didn't have decisions to make. But now we treasure this opportunity to help those in need.

For thirty-one years I had the privilege of living with a man who never said never. During his last years when he was working on the national campus of the Good Samaritan Society, and aiming at making it a world-class teaching and learning center for long-term care, he saw no reason why I. M. Pei couldn't be the architect for such a project.

At times he had to settle for far less than his dreams. Other times the projects he had in mind failed miserably. But much of what he envisioned happened. His belief in aiming high and dreaming big dreams was something he lived and shared with us, his family. I can only imagine the dreaming he is doing now.

Prayer

20 "I pray not only for them, but also for those who believe in me because of their message. 21 I pray that they may all be one. Father! May they be in us, just as you are in me and I am in you. May they be one, so that the world will believe that you sent me. 22 I gave them the same glory you gave me, so that they may be one, just as you and I are one: 23 I in them and you in me, so that they may be completely one, in order that the world may know that you sent me and that you love them as you love me. 24 Father! You have given them to me, and I want them to be with me where I am, so that they may see my glory, the glory you gave me; for you loved me before the world was made. 25 Righteous Father! The world does not know you, but I know you, and these know that you sent me. 26 I made you known to them, and I will continue to do so, in order that the love you have for me may be in them, and so that I also may be in them." John 17:20-26

7 "Ask, and you will receive; seek, and you will find; knock, and the door will be opened to you." Matthew 7:7

About a half a dozen years ago I was sitting in my office, and there was a little knock on the door. "Come!" I said. The door opened, and she walked in. She was one of my favorite students—bright and able to recognize as few others could those little witticisms and points of insight that came from the campus pastor's mouth.

Sit down," I said, and she did. "What can I do for you?" She started to talk about light things. And then she looked at me, and tears spilled out of her eyes.

She said, "Pastor, I just can't pray anymore."

I thought about her this past week as I pored over this Gospel text of Jesus praying to his father on behalf of all those who believe in him, not just his disciples. Reading the Greek you see that this prayer and those disciples have a timeless quality.

He prayed not only for those who at that moment believed in him, but for all those who would believe in him. Think about it. At that time, Jesus was praying for you. He was praying for all of us.

I thought about that student as I picked up one of my favorite authors, Abraham Heschel. While reading, I came across a little statement of his from his last book, *A Passion for Truth*. He said this: "It is easier to study than to pray; it is harder to become a God-fearing person than a scholar."

I met him once when I was in graduate school at a Jewish community center. In the midst of his talk, he asked for a glass of water. Someone brought it to him.

You have to think of this kind of dingy, big old building with a bunch of Hasidic Jews and a few other onlookers. There on the stage, before he took a drink of water, he bowed his head in prayer to give thanks. And as he did, I heard someone behind me lean over and whisper, "Phony!"

He did not know Abraham Heschel, for nothing could have been further from his mind than to *not* give thanks to God—the God who created the universe and the world and fire and water—for the gift of life. And for a glass of water.

I thought about Heschel, and I thought about that girl, and I thought about this text. I thought about the life of prayer. Another text came to my mind: *"Ask, and you will receive; seek, and you will find; knock"*—and that is the climax—*"knock, and the door will be opened to you."* Now, what an image of prayer that is: *"Knock."*

Prayer is not weak and limp-wristed. When you knock you have to have your hand in a fist. What a powerful image. Not some sentimental walk in the garden with God. Prayer is much more profound, much more in the trenches of day-to-day life. Jesus invites us to respond to life as it is by praying, and in prayer asking, seeking, and knocking.

I think of those beautiful little Gospel stories that we hear. Luke tells them so well. One was the story of a woman who pled her case before the unjust judge. He denied her many times, but in the end, because she would not give up, he finally granted her petition.

There is the story of the friend who came to another's house at midnight because sudden visitors had come and he needed something to feed them. He pounded on that door. The friend told him to go away, that everything was buttoned up for the night, and he was in bed with his wife and kids.

I can see his point; he probably spent two or three hours trying to get everyone to bed, including the animals, and now to crawl out, wake everyone up, help this friend, and then get everyone back to bed—it was too much! He said, "No."

The man kept knocking until he finally relented.

"Even so," says Jesus, *"how much more will your Father in heaven give to those who ask."* A beautiful little picture of prayer.

I share with you a Hasidic story.

An old rabbi used to spend much of his time praying for those who were deep sinners and asking for God's forgiveness. And God would always forgive. Until finally there was one whose sins were so heinous that God said, "No."

And then, the story goes, the rabbi stamped his foot, and God immediately forgave that man. The story goes on. Only a father or a mother can understand this story. Do you remember the first time your child stamped his foot at you? How delighted you were! It can only happen the first time, and only once. Just so was God delighted with the rabbi.

There's something about this whole picture of prayer that invites us to never give up, to come before him, to pray. I see examples of the power of prayer everywhere.

I have a friend who used to live in Chicago and has now come to South Dakota to pastor a rural church.

"What's going on in your life?" I asked him several years ago. "What's the key theology you're studying?"

"Well," he said, "this might surprise you, but it's prayer. I'm a yoke-fellow, a prayer partner, with a man out in New York City. We get together twice a year, we pray daily, we write to each other. My life is based on prayer. It's the key."

Ask – seek – knock. I invite you to be people whose life, whose foundation, whose very core of existence, is founded on, based on, built on, a life of prayer.

Are you depressed? Do what you can to help yourself. Go to see a counselor. And pray! Are you worried about your work? Be creative, and pour yourself into it. And pray! Are you worried about what is going to happen next? Jobs? The future? Give your worry to the Lord in prayer.

Are you wondering about that relationship—if it's right, if it's going the way it should? Stop and pray! Not just words mumbled, hoping maybe something might get through, but ask, seek, knock and never give up. Be tenacious as a bulldog. If someone has prayed for you today, you will never know what that prayer will do, how it may change the course of your life?

The key is prayer. For he has promised that whoever asks will receive; whoever seeks will find; and if you knock, the very gates of heaven will be opened unto you.

Reflection

Several things jump out at me from this sermon. I never thought about the fact that Jesus is referring to more than just the disciples when he petitions God for his people, but he is also including us. The concept that Jesus asked the Father to include us as his and for his spirit to be in us is so monumental it pierces my heart.

The biblical stories of praying and never giving up resonate with me. They appeal to my stubbornness and tenacity and speak a word of hope for any situation.

I know so well what Heschel is speaking of when he says it is much easier to be a student than a God-fearing person. The times I have paused to pray and then had my mind wander are countless. Does it ever not happen is the question. Have I prayed long enough and hard enough?

Jesus teaches the disciples a simple, short prayer: the Lord's Prayer. We are told the Spirit intercedes for us when we are at a loss for words. Some God-fearing people pray by saying Jesus' name over and over, almost as if they were in a trance.

I believe God wants us to pray continuously, always being open to God speaking to us or directing us. Sometimes we forget that prayer is not just talking to God. Having said that, I also know how difficult it is to remember to pray without ceasing, and some days I forget to pray altogether.

And then there are the questions. When I think about prayer and the power of prayer, how can I keep from wondering if God was listening to the countless people who prayed for Mark after he was diagnosed with cancer? Why are some prayers answered and not others?

The answer I have given myself is that God hears our prayers, that all our prayers are answered, but the answer is not always what we want to hear. Although the doctors thought Mark might die in a few weeks, he lived for five and a half months. That time, although difficult, was a gift for all of us. Mark was able to finish all his business as the President and CEO of Good Samaritan, and he was able to take care of his family business as well. Most importantly, we had time to talk about everything.

Our children visited often and spent endless hours talking with their father. Multitudes of people were able to visit Mark, and they shared moments of deep faith and love together. Mark talked with me about my future, which was intensely difficult at the time, but proved to be important. As death became imminent, I was tortured by conflicting feelings. I wanted him to be done with suffering, but I couldn't bear the thought of losing him. Once again God answered prayers by giving me a sense of peacefulness after Mark died.

Another gift during that time was the Celebration of Life service the Good Samaritan Society had for Mark. Good Samaritan workers, community folks, church friends, and old friends came together to tell Mark how much they loved him and what he had meant to them during his life. It was like being at your own funeral. How many people get to have that before they die?!

Mark, who had always been one to ignore what was going on with his body and to focus on others, was able to go to work every day until two weeks before he died. A gift from the medical professionals and a miracle from God.

His dying paralleled Holy Week so closely that it didn't seem like a random happening. On Maundy Thursday, his doctor visited his mother and me as we sat at his bedside. Mark seemed to be comatose. The doctor thought he would die very soon, perhaps that evening.

But the next evening, Good Friday, Pastor Brian Mortenson came for a visit, and with his booming voice announced to Mark that it was Good Friday, and he wanted to have a prayer with him. Mark responded, becoming alert and animated.

The next morning, as we were lying together, I suddenly remembered I had not told him what a magnificent job he had done during his illness of modeling faith and hope for the life to come. I called his name twice and asked him to listen to me. Again, he became alert, and I know he heard my message.

About 8 p.m. on Saturday night, hours before Easter Sunday, Mark breathed his last breath. I gathered our family members around his bed and shared a prayer together. We finally went home, a place that would seem bereft of his dynamic presence for many years to come. There we saw an unusual comet, its many points of light stretched out across the sky beaming down brightly. I pictured Mark riding right on top.

One of the things I discovered early on about Mark was that he was always able to get tickets for the best seats to anything, and he got them at the last minute so they were relatively inexpensive. He also had a talent for being able to get into concerts or appearances before anyone else. He was persistent in seeking and knocking until the door was opened. And, I believe, he did it again.

Though I love my life dearly, I believe Heaven is real, and that our spirits head there the minute they leave the body. I have read many accounts of people who have been able to "visit" heaven, and their stories are amazing. I do believe we will be with God and will experience life and love in a way that is beyond comparison to anything we know here. True to form, Mark got there first, blessed by the stubborn prayers of those of us who loved him and drawn by the power of the Savior he loved.

We Are All Brothers and Sisters in Suffering

3 More than that, we rejoice in our sufferings, knowing that suffering produces endurance, 4 and endurance produces character, and character produces hope, 5 and hope does not disappoint us, because God's love has been poured into our hearts through the Holy Spirit which has been given to us. Romans 5:3-5 RSV

She was a world famous singer, giving concerts mainly in the United States and Europe. Often she would accompany herself on her lute which she had had crafted years before by the best in the world. After one concert, she noticed that the sound board had cracked. She was distraught. She carefully packed her lute and flew to the old man who had so carefully built her instrument.

"Yes, it could be repaired," he assured her. And then he said these words: "Now your lute will speak with its own unique voice. It is only after its sound board, its heart, has been broken and carefully repaired that it sings most beautifully."

A careful examination of great violins

Elizabeth Jerstad

of the world shows, I understand, that the sound board has been cracked and carefully repaired on most of them, including many of the great violins made by Antonio Stradivari, and even the finest violin in the world, the Alard Strad. The Messiah Strad, though, has never been broken, and the great violinists wonder how beautiful it will sound when it too breaks and is repaired.

I wonder if there isn't a little parable about life, growth, suffering, and most of all, grace, in all of this. I have noticed that some of the deepest love I have been given, the most understanding, compassion, forgiveness, kindness, deepest camaraderie I have shared has come from folks whose hearts have been broken and carefully mended. From people who have known suffering, who have walked through the valley of the shadow, who have experienced personal failure, loss, brokenness, or death.

It is not the suffering that makes the difference, though. Ann Morrow Lindberg once said: "Everybody suffers. Suffering won't make you any better. But suffering mixed together with love and patience and understanding and a continued vulnerability—that can lead to a new birth." And, I might add, a unique voice that speaks and sings most beautifully.

Now, there is a key to all of this, this broken heart and beautiful music. St. Paul put his finger on it; *we rejoice in our sufferings, knowing that suffering produces endurance, and endurance produces character, and character produces hope, and hope does not disappoint us, because God's love has been poured into our hearts through the Holy Spirit which has been give to us.*

The Psalmist knew it: *"Though I walk through the valley of the shadow of death, I will fear no evil, for Thou art with me."* Words of Jesus: "I will be with you always…" There it is! It is he who initiates the healing, the caring, the coping—he who surrounds us with love and understanding. God's love has been poured into our hearts through the Holy Spirit (God with us), which has been given to us.

We are all brothers and sisters in suffering. Our sound boards have been cracked or will be, our hearts broken or will be. But know this: our suffering can be an occasion for growth, for renewal, for new sensitivity to others, and for greater reliance on our Lord, the Christ Jesus, whose life and death and new life is the most beautiful song of all. And he invites us to let that song of love, hope and joy, of caring, sharing, and kindness, and of forgiveness, reverberate off our sounding boards, broken, but lovingly repaired by him for the sake of others.

Reflection

Today is the 14th anniversary of Mark's death. My kids have written to each other and to me with amusing stories about their dad, but also poignant words about missing him. Sarah wrote: "Thinking about Dad a lot today, it's hard to believe it's been 14 years. I was remembering today getting picked up or dropped off by Dad often in the DeLorean—at school, at the roller skating rink. I even remember riding home from the cabin to Sioux Falls sharing the front seat with Jenny Byrne the whole way! He loved that car. I also remember his affinity for sugar free popsicles. My favorite memory that came to mind was when he got the giggles during our family church photo session. I sure miss him."

Mike wrote: "I always laugh when I think about his various health kicks: niacin (where he OD'd and turned orange), those stretching exercises with that hot silver body suit, that little circular jogger thing... He was definitely an "all in" guy. That's why so many of the things he worked on were successful. I miss him too, and if he came down from heaven right now to sit next to me and have a conversation, I know it would be as if we hadn't missed a beat. It seems like I just saw him yesterday, when I think about him."

Rachel shared a story about when he had dropped by her apartment in Minneapolis, and she had given him a strawberry-rhubarb pie to take home—his favorite. He said he was on a diet and shouldn't eat any but would take it home. He called her a half an hour later to say he had pulled over on the shoulder and eaten half the pie, and that it was the best pie he had ever tasted.

Last night a woman told me she was a student at Augustana when he was the campus pastor there, and that she loved his sermons. I hear others say from time to time: "I knew Mark. He was a wonderful man." Each remembrance is a gift to me and brings that person closer to my heart.

At this point, remembering Mark is an uplifting, sweet experience. But the first five years were difficult to say the least. I had to come to terms with losing my partner, who was my best friend, my favorite companion, and the father of our children. During those first years I learned that real grieving is real suffering.

Suffering in silence or alone is the worst. During the first few years after his death I know I sometimes blocked out the reality that he was gone. I know I tried to be strong and independent and get through this on my own. At times I didn't know if I would get through the next minute, but God seemed to reach out to me then with a person or persons who either understood my grief or took me away from myself. My softball team was good at that. At practice, when I was down, their energy and love picked me up.

I believe some of our best moments are spent sharing the struggles of another, and supporting that person. If we have been down that road ourselves, we are more apt to feel comfortable listening and reaching out to another who is suffering. Death and depression are not topics that everyone feels comfortable talking about, but those who have been there can speak a word of hope.

A few years ago my friend Kevin achieved sobriety after many years of substance abuse. In his gratitude, he has shaped a treatment facility based on the Twelve-Step Program, established five group homes where recovering addicts can live with others who are struggling, and formed an organization to bring the problem out in the open. The premise is that no one should have to face addiction alone or hide it in shame.

Real suffering in this case produced a strong man with character who is giving hope to those who struggle with substance abuse and to their families and friends. Anyone who has been down that path has most likely felt as though they were walking in the valley of the shadow of death. The strong message is that they don't have to continue hiding and heading downward. A hand of help and healing is there for them.

A big, strong Augustana football player talked to me today about suffering from depression. Don't be fooled if things look all right on the surface. If you listen you will hear that cry for help. If you look closely, you will see the person who is hurting. When we share in the suffering and keep hope alive, it helps both the one who has suffered and the one who is suffering.

Sometimes we need that outstretched hand. Sometimes we are the arms that lift people up. And always we are able to be the lifting arms because we were once the one who needed to be lifted up.

None of us chooses to suffer. But, St. Paul is right, strength comes through suffering. Hope is born in suffering. And believing that suffering has meaning and purpose can make it bearable.

What Happens After Death?

1 "Do not be worried and upset," Jesus told them. "Believe in God and believe also in me. 2 There are many rooms in my Father's house, and I am going to prepare a place for you. I would not tell you this if it were not so. 3 And after I go and prepare a place for you, I will come back and take you to myself, so that you will be where I am. 4 You know the way that leads to the place where I am going." 5 Thomas said to him, "Lord, we do not know where you are going; so how can we know the way to get there?" 6 Jesus answered him, "I am the way, the truth, and the life; no one goes to the Father except by me. 7 Now that you have known me," he said to them, "you will know my Father also, and from now on you do know him and you have seen him." John 14:1-7

12 Now, since our message is that Christ has been raised from death, how can some of you say that the dead will not be raised to life? 13 If that is true, it means that Christ was not raised; 14 and if Christ has not been raised from death, then we have nothing to preach and you have nothing to believe. 15 More than that, we are shown to be lying about God, because we said that he raised Christ from death—but if it is true that the dead are not raised to life, then he did not raise Christ. 16 For if the dead are not raised, neither has Christ been raised. 17 And if Christ has not been raised, then your faith is a delusion and you are still lost in your sins. 18 It would also mean that the believers in Christ who have died are lost. 19 If our hope in Christ is good for this life only and no more, then we deserve more pity than anyone else in all the world. 1 Corinthians 15:12-19

What will happen to you when you die? Have you ever thought about that? You haven't?! You really need help! I think it is the most common thought that spins its way around our minds and in our fantasies, from early on until we take our last breath. What will happen to you when you die?

There are a myriad of answers one could come up with. I suspect there are as many answers as there are people. Each of us has our own thoughts and questions about it. And I suspect we struggle, wondering. Are we not oftentimes, in the deep and dark places of the night, haunted by those fears about what will happen? We are hit with the realization of our own finiteness, of the realization that, as the Psalms say, *"No man lives who will not see death. We will all die in the blink of an eye."*

I suspect I will be an old guy, walking around with my walker in the nursing home, chasing the nurses. And then I will be gone, just like that. It was not that long ago that I celebrated my tenth birthday. I will never forget it—I got my first big red bike. And now, thirty years later, it still seems like it was yesterday. Time flies! Before we know it, our children are grown, and we are well on the way to becoming old. But we still struggle with the question: What will happen when we die?

It has been interesting for me as a pastor and as a theologian, to take a look at how the Church and how Christian people at different times in their history, even in our recent history, deal with the question of what will happen to us after we die. I recall when I was in the seminary. It was a time of strong and powerful focus on social concern. There was the "Death of God" movement going on. Many of my professors talked about the fact that, really, what is important is not what happens to you after you die. When we die, that may be all there is. Of primary importance is what you do with your life here on earth.

Now, I had to agree that what we do with our life here on earth is very important—no question about that. But I also had to say with St. Paul, *"If beyond this life there is no hope, then we, of all people, are most to be pitied."* Truly there must be something more. Then he continued, *"But thanks be to God who gives us the promise of everlasting life."* What happens to us after we die?

There is a strain running through the whole biblical message that comes at us from our future and penetrates our now. This is what we call an eschatological promise, a promise that beyond this life there is something more, a gift that is given to us who are God's children and who believe in him. We are people of promise. We live in the hope and the promise given to us by God himself through Jesus Christ, that beyond this life we will be ushered into a new kingdom, another kingdom. That is my hope for each one of us.

The invitation of the Gospel is this: You are invited to risk everything on that promise, to stake every breath of your life on the promise and on the hope that it is absolutely true. The invitation itself, given to us by Christ, and our response to this invitation, our saying "yes" in the face of all that would dissuade us, the world and the doubts from within, invokes fear.

Chaim Potok in his latest book called *The Book of Lights* speaks of our doubts in this way: it is "the silken whisper from the dark side" that haunts us with the possibility of nothingness, with the possibility of meaninglessness, with the possibility that this is all there is. The Gospel invites us, even in the face of that—the tempter, the deceiver—to risk everything on the hope that the promise is true.

Are you willing to do it? Are you willing to give your life up, to give it away to Jesus, and by doing that to give it away to one another? Are you willing to make that leap of faith and of trust? The very answer in your heart of hearts of "yes" is sign and symbol that

God's Spirit is here with us. For we cannot confess, even believe, unless God's Spirit works within us and creates the opening we call faith. Believe it. It is true. Risk everything on it. You will have life.

For you, all my saints, there is a gift and there is a promise worthy of your giving up all. That is the promise that we will have eternal life. And God himself will be with us. He will wipe away every tear from our eyes, and *"there will be no more sorrow, no more mourning, no more fear, no more death. For behold,"* he says, *"I make all things new."* Children of the promise, saints of God, rejoice. God's kingdom is with you. And we celebrate that today in the feast of victory that is the down payment of that which is to come for us: a life filled with love, with oneness with God, a life without end.

Reflection

Throughout typing this sermon, I could not help but think of Mark's dying and death, and what happened afterwards. During his illness the emotions of grief and hope made my heart and throat ache. Toward the end, I could hardly stand to watch him continue to suffer, but neither could I stand to think of life without him. When all the tubes and machines were finally wheeled away, I crawled into bed with him and held him close, softly telling him he was going to the arms of God, and that we would be OK.

During his illness he was insistent that our family be free to express emotions of grief and anger over his illness and diagnosis of late stage colon cancer. I am so grateful for the five and a half months we had together. One wintry weekend when Mike, Kelly, and Sarah were home and Mark was not feeling well, we all crawled into our big bed together and spent the entire weekend there, sleeping, talking, praying, crying, eating, watching movies, and telling jokes. It was such a bittersweet time, but a time I am so thankful for.

On another cold night in February, I crawled into bed late,

and Mark was so quiet I wondered if he was still breathing. I sat staring at him, trying to detect a breath until he finally opened one eye and said, "Why don't you lie down so we can both get some sleep."

One December day following Mark's death, I attended church and heard the news that Fred, a dear friend and colleague of Mark's, was diagnosed with inoperable brain cancer. I thought about going to the hospital to see him, but decided it should be a private family time. Besides, I didn't know him as well as Mark had.

Later that afternoon, I found myself in the car driving to the hospital, as though an unseen force had put me there. Once in his room, I sat down on the bed, and Fred looked at me and said, "I don't know if I should tell you this, and I have struggled with whether to share this with you, but I am going to tell you now." He cleared his throat and paused. Fred was the kind of guy who was all about the present and what he could see and read and hear.

He proceeded to tell me what happened when he got to Mark's memorial service a few minutes late. "I walked into the narthex, and there, across the room, stood Mark, smiling at me his huge smile. He had his navy blue suit on and looked great. I just stared at him, and finally glanced down. When I looked again, he was gone. I didn't know what to make of this, and I didn't know if I should tell you about it."

A few months later, Fred died. I know why I found myself going to the hospital that day. I know why Fred told me the story. Sometimes our doubts and fears need some help. I no longer had to think about Mark in his cold, wintry grave. He was at his own memorial service, sending a welcoming assurance to his friend who would soon join him.

The Greatest Gift

Let us love one another, for love comes from God. Whoever loves is a child of God and knows God. Whoever does not love, does not know God, for God is love. This is what love is. It is not that we have loved God, but that He loved us and sent his Son that we might have life. This is how he showed his love to us. He sent his son so that our sins might be forgiven. Dear friends, if God so loved us, then we should love one another. 1 John 4:7-11

From 1st Corinthians, Chapter 13: *If I have not love, I have nothing.*

From the 15th Chapter of the Gospel of St. John, these words: *Greater love has no man than this, that a man lay down his life for his friends.*

I have the most delightful children. Some days, frankly, I'd sell them all down the river real cheap, but sometimes they capture my heart and give me a feeling of such warmth that it overwhelms me.

Today I had the best visit with my youngest daughter Sarah. She came in early this morning and sat down in my study where I was doing a little work and just started to talk. And we laughed and talked and I loved it. I'm still basking in the glow of our visit. As I was walking over to the chapel, I started to reminisce about her.

I remember one summer day at our cabin when Sarah was about four. The water around the dock is deep, so the rule at the cabin is you have to be able to jump off the end of the dock and swim to the shore and back before you can be on the dock without your life jacket on. Mike and Rachel had passed the test, but not Sarah.

On this day, Sarah kept running out on the dock without her life jacket. Finally I said to myself, "She's going to fall in and we might lose her." I thought I'd better scare her to shape her up a bit. The next time she went down without her life jacket on, I stormed down, got a stern look on my face, and said, "Sarah!! Get off the dock without your life jacket on!!"

I scooped her up and stomped back up the dock to the deck. I glanced at her face and saw it was filled with terror. Just as I thought I had made my point, she peed all over me. I just scared it right out of her. She won.

But we got things squared away, and later on that day, I was lying out on the beach reading. Sarah was playing in the sand beside me. She started to rub her hands up and down my chest. She looked at me and said, "Daddy, I like all your feathers."

She used my chest for a pillow, and snuggled in for a nap. All of a sudden, she popped up, looked at me and said, "I can tell you have Jesus in your heart 'cause I hear him bumping around in there." How I love her, and each of my children.

The greatest gift we have is the gift of love. Sometimes that gift of love is given, or not, in the midst of the messiness of our lives. Listen to two stories about love, and reflect on your own potential for love.

I was sitting in my office when I received a phone call. It was a young man, a preacher's son, whom I had known for most of his 20 years. The first thing he said to me was, "Pastor Jerstad, I'm down at the jail. Can you come and see me?" I said, "I'll be right down." It was about 11:30 at night.

At the jail, an officer let me in. The door clanged coldly behind me as the jailer led me to a cell. We sat down to visit. "I've been busted for selling drugs," he said. "I know I shouldn't do it. If I had it to do all over again, I would never even touch the stuff. But the worst part is this: My dad's a preacher and I'm afraid to call home because he's going to disown me. I don't think he'll even come to see me. How can he do anything but hate me?"

I said, "You'd better call." He made the call home, and there was silence on the other end of the phone. Then he heard his dad say, "I'll be there." He was scared stiff. About half an hour later, we heard those big footsteps coming down the hall of that county prison. The jailer opened the door and his dad came in. He didn't say, "Are you guilty?" He didn't say, "How could you possibly have done this? Don't you know that I'm probably going to be kicked out of my parish because of this? What kind of a kid are you?"

His dad just stood there and looked at his son and then held out his arms. The son stood up, all 6 feet 5 inches of him, and they embraced. All his dad said was, "Son, I love you."

I know that was an expensive love. I walked the streets of that town. I heard what people said. Behind his back and to his face. He patiently listened and would say, "I know. It's all true. But he's my son, and I love him." A picture of love without counting the cost. Love comes from God.

That is the greatest gift of love and the greatest love of all, the greatest love story: Jesus Christ loves you so much that he walks down the halls of your heart and sees you for who you really are. He doesn't turn away or say, "Yuck! I don't like what you've done. I don't like your story. I don't like who you are."

He holds out his arms through time and space, and with love and forgiveness reaches out to grab you and make you his own. Each day Christ offers us the greatest gift of all, the gift of love. There is power in that gift, a profound power that touches peoples' lives and changes things.

This was the power of love in action poignantly told to me by a friend after he visited a camp for delinquent teenage boys on the shore of Lake Superior. Many of the kids come from Chicago, ages 15 and 16. On his tour was a small stone chapel.

He walked into the chapel and was immediately face to face with two pictures of former campers. Rosy was a black-haired, brown-eyed black kid with a big smile on his face. On the other side was another picture of a blue-eyed kid with an equally big smile, whose name was Rick.

My friend asked the director of the camp, "Why are these kids' pictures here? Did their parents contribute to the chapel?" The director smiled and said, "No, but let me tell you the story about Rosy and Rick." And he proceeded to tell the following story.

The previous year, Rosy and Rick had come to camp from Chicago, and met each other shortly after camp started. They became close friends immediately, and in three short weeks, they were as close as brothers. They followed each other around and talked to each other late into the evening.

One weekend, they went on a canoe trip on Lake Superior. About noon the group they were with pulled into an island and got ready to set up camp. While some of the boys got busy setting up tents, Rick spotted something bobbing in the water, and, curious to see what it was, pushed a canoe out and paddled toward the object.

Before he could reach it, a Lake Superior storm blew in quickly from the north, causing huge waves with white caps to kick up. Rick's canoe capsized, and he went under. Up he came, hanging onto the canoe and screaming for help.

Two counselors ran to a canoe and started pushing it toward the lake. Rosy was just as quick and announced, "I'm coming, too." He hopped into the canoe and the three of them paddled out together. But before they could quite reach Rick, their canoe capsized as well. All three surfaced and hung onto their canoe.

The wind was howling and rain was pouring down, combining with dark clouds to cause limited visibility. They yelled, "Hang on Rick, hang on!"

Rick yelled back, "I can't!" He slipped underneath the surface, but came back up and grabbed for the canoe again. Rosy screamed, "Rick, I'm coming. Hang on!" He pushed away from the canoe, and those frail, little skinny black arms cut through the water with the strength of a man four times his age.

He got to Rick just as Rick slipped off the canoe. He desperately reached out and grabbed his friend, and Rick grabbed him back. They were both pulled underneath the water.

The counselors, fortunately, were swept to shore. They searched the shoreline all afternoon and into the evening. Finally they found the bodies of Rick and Rosy against the shoreline, still holding each other close.

Rick and Rosy will be remembered forever by the words written under their pictures in the chapel. "Ricky, who was loved enough to have a friend give him his life." "Rosy, who loved enough to pay that price."

"Greater love has no one than this, that he give his life for his friends." Jesus has given his life for you. He invites you to find the deepest, most profound meaning in the life he has given to you. He challenges us all to spend ourselves in love for each other, without counting the cost. *"Faith, hope, and love abide, but the greatest of these is love."*

Reflection

One of the reasons that Mark's sermons have staying power is that he always used stories to illustrate his points. Sometimes the stories were about common, everyday events, and sometimes they were quite dramatic. They were sometimes a bit embellished, which used to bother me, until I realized that a little embellishment helped the story make its point and made it more memorable.

Mark was a lover—of his life, his friends, his work, his family, his God. Although he was reflective and a dreamer, he also put his dreams into action. And yet, he seemed to find time to pay attention to the people in his life, whether he knew them well or not.

While I all too often have allowed expediency—getting the job done, focusing on the result—to remove me from deeply listening to others and to paying attention to their feelings, Mark was the opposite. I learned from him, as he took time to listen to other peoples' stories and share a good laugh with them.

That is love in action. Sometimes it takes so little to show love. Sometimes just a smile, or holding the door open, or calling someone by name can make a difference in the other person's life. Mother Teresa talked about that: "We cannot all do great things, but we can do little things with great love."

Inspired, I decide I want to be good at loving. I make a list of thoughtful things to do for my family and for others, not expecting anything in return. I do them and check them all off my list. There, God, I did good today.

God smiles at this feeble attempt and, I hope, accepts it anyway. I do believe this: If I take time in the morning to thank God for my life, my family, this beautiful world, and his great act of redeeming love by giving us his only son, my gratitude will push me out the door to do, in love, whatever I can, wherever I can, with whomever I meet.

We first met Rick at the cabin, when we needed some carpentry work done. We liked him right away. He was unbelievably good and fast at his job and had a ready smile. We became close friends and eventually hired him to look after our cabin, when we weren't around, and invited him to use it as if it were his own.

When Rick's father died in his fifties of a heart attack, Rick asked Mark to preside over the service at the funeral home and at the distribution of ashes. Since Rick's dad was a fishing guide on Rainy Lake, the funeral procession was a line-up of 14 boats, following each other on a five-mile ride up Rainy Lake to the spot where he used to have a cabin. Part of the service was Rick riding in a seaplane, which came in low, distributing his father's ashes onto the lake.

When Mark died, there was a memorial service following a private family interment. Our Savior's Lutheran Church was packed—about 800 people. Afterwards, I spent hours in the church basement talking with friends and family. At one point, I glanced over to a table where one man was sitting alone. It was Rick. He had driven 500 miles by himself to say goodbye to Mark and to be of comfort to me. What a gift of love!

We all receive them, these gifts in our lives, little and big acts of love. Even when acts of love are done grudgingly by us or by others, God still honors them and uses them for the well being of the world.

As we consciously attempt to be more loving in our daily lives, perhaps a good place to start is with our family. Just because we have known someone our whole life, or we are married to him or her, doesn't mean we can be mean or careless or disrespectful. On the contrary, being loving toward our family members, in whatever little and big ways we can, even during times of great tension and disagreement, not only creates a loving family, but it can also help us practice loving kindness—an attitude and a skill we can then bring to the rest of our world.

The mother of my daughter-in-law, Kelly, spends endless hours helping Mike and Kelly with childcare, sometimes caring for all four of the children. Recently she took care of the two-year-old twins for seven days and nights, so the parents could spend significant time with their two older children. An act of loving kindness.

Kelly's grandmother, Vi, never missed a night rocking the twins to sleep for the first year of their lives. Her daily routine included arriving at Mike and Kelly's house around 5 p.m., helping feed the twins, picking up after everyone, doing dishes, and helping put the twins to bed. A litany of love in action.

Jesus reminded us we could be stewards of love anywhere, anytime: *"If you do it for those who are the least important in society, you are doing it for me."* The secret is to ask God daily for the gift of love, of being loving. His promise is clear: *"Ask and you shall receive."*

Help me, O God, to always remember your love for me and all your people and to pass that love on each day, whenever and wherever I can. Amen

Letters of Love

4 But God's mercy is so abundant, and his love for us is so great, 5 that while we were spiritually dead in our disobedience he brought us to life with Christ. It is by God's grace that you have been saved. 6 In our union with Christ Jesus he raised us up with him to rule with him in the heavenly world. 7 He did this to demonstrate for all time to come the extraordinary greatness of his grace in the love he showed us in Christ Jesus. 8 For it is by God's grace that you have been saved through faith. It is not the result of your own efforts, 9 but God's gift, so that no one can boast about it. 10 God has made us what we are, and in our union with Christ Jesus he has created us for a life of good deeds, which he has already prepared for us to do. Ephesians 2:4-10

And from Ephesians 3:14-21: *14 For this reason I fall on my knees before the Father, 15 from whom every family in heaven and on earth receives its true name. 16 I ask God from the wealth of his glory to give you power through his Spirit to be strong in your inner selves, 17 and I pray that Christ will make his home in your hearts through faith. I pray that you may have your roots and foundation in love, 18 so that you, together with all God's people, may have the power to understand how broad and long, how high and deep, is Christ's love. 19 Yes, may you come to know his love—although it can never be fully known—and so be completely filled with the very nature of God. 20 To him who by means of his power working in us is able to do so much more than we can ever ask for, or even think of: 21 to God be the glory in the church and in Christ Jesus for all time, forever and ever! Amen.*

I've seen it happen often. Sitting in the campus coffee shop, I notice. Down the stairs comes a coed, putting on her coat. She passes the bookstore and then walks by that row upon row of PO boxes. And, ever so casually, she just happens to glance over to see if anything is in there. We can all imagine what happens next.

Between classes, she just happens to find herself in the Commons again. And as she casually walks by, happens to drop her pencil. She picks it up and looks over to see if maybe it is there. Lunchtime. Now she can just look, because everyone else is, so she gets right down and checks it out again. This time, she sees it sitting at an angle. She pulls open the door, doesn't bother with locking it—takes too much time with the combination—and shuts it.

Her first urge when she sees who it's from is to rip it open and read it right there. Then she thinks, no, I don't want to do it here. She thinks about that favorite couch of hers over in the library, tucked away by the window. She can postpone her meal for just a bit, and she skips over to the library. She says, "Hi" to everybody, I mean, she genuinely says, "Hi," walks in, goes upstairs, sits down, and gets comfortable. Carefully, she opens it up and takes it out. It's from him. And she's in love. And it's pure joy.

She reads it, not just once, but again and again and again, and she reads sections over several times. She loves the way he always signs his letters, and she knows it is a little weird, but she holds it right up next to her for a moment, and she can feel a touch. She's in love. She's just received a love letter, and she carries those words with her throughout the day, stopping several times to read it again. The last thing she does before she falls asleep is to read that letter one more time.

You may be thinking, I wish I could get that kind of love letter. But you have, and you do, on a daily basis! Our Lord himself has written a series of love letters to those of us whom he loves dearly. His letters have come to us in many forms. They have come to us through his word, giving us the opportunity to approach that book as though it were a letter from one who loves us. What a gift!

His letters of love come to us through bread and wine, the sacraments, and as we receive that bread and wine, we receive Christ himself, another mysterious word of love. Those letters of love come to us, and have come to us through friends who show their care and concern. We sit before a magnificent letter of love, written to us in love, about love, attempting to inspire love. What a gift!

The life of the church is centered around letters of love from him who loves us. Those love letters aren't going to do us much good if we don't open up our POs, pull them out, and read them. It doesn't mean that we are loved any less. His love for us will never flag. But the way we tie in, the way we grow, is through reading those letters of love, experiencing them, and that is the invitation of the Gospel for us now and always.

Love letters inspire us. They do something to us. They change us. I think of my wife, Sandy, and I smile, because she still sends me love letters. They do something to me, the letters I receive now. In some ways, they do more than they did all those years ago when we were courting.

These letters of love, sent in love, for us, through Jesus Christ our Savior, do something to us. They change us, make us his, and turn us loose to be agents of that love, to be little letters of love in the lives of all those whom God places in our path.

My friends, it is my prayer that you will realize that your POs are stuffed, filled with letters of love from our Lord Jesus Christ. I invite you to open those letters, and to read them until they're sweaty, until they're all wrinkled up, until they're yours, until you know every word by heart.

I invite you to respond to those letters of love, sharing that love selflessly, never counting the cost, with all those whom your life is called to touch, in the name of our Lord.

I pray you may have your roots and foundations in love, so you, together with all God's people, may have the power to understand how broad and long, how high and deep is Christ's love.

To him, who by means of his power working in us, is able to do so much more than we can ever ask for, or even think of, to God be the glory in the Church and in Christ Jesus for all time, forever and ever.

Reflection

This sermon brings to mind all the letters we hand-wrote to each other during the time we were dating and then engaged. I remember the joy and excitement of getting a letter from Mark. The shiver that went up and down my body. His passion and love for life came through his handwriting, exciting and thrilling me about us and our future together.

I was stunned recently to find some letters my father had written to my mother early on in their marriage. While I always knew how close they were and how deeply they loved one another, it was a brand new experience to read about that commitment penned from my father's own hand. Love letters have a strange ability to jump right off the page and grab someone's heart.

My friend Linda asked me not too long ago how much I continue to think of Mark. "Not a day goes by that I don't think of him," I say, "but it is more like I am connected to him in a way that transcends life itself." He is woven into my thinking and doing, not always consciously, but never far away. Being able to edit and publish his sermons brought forth an amazing sense of connection. I can hear him talk, feel his presence, and see his smiling face. As Mark used to say, "What a gift!"

If I wrote a letter to Mark right now, it might look like this:

June 2011

Dear Mark,

Fourteen years have passed since you died and moved on to the next world. Yet you live on in my heart and in the hearts and minds of your children and sometimes your grandchildren. Yes, your grandchildren. The ones you always wanted to hold and admire and toss up into the air. While I feel you are still closely connected to us, I am not sure how much you are aware of what goes on around here, so let me tell you about them.

Your oldest grandchild is Sarah, born August 7, 1997. At least you saw a picture of her when she was in the womb, and commented, "what a miracle!" And she certainly has been. She is fourteen and beautiful, with your deep blue eyes, your eyebrows, and the Jerstad face. She also looks a lot like her namesake, Aunt Sarah, your daughter. Rachel kids her sister about how unfair that is, but there she is! She has a delightful personality, quiet at times, but a real leader in school with her friends. She is in ninth grade and is getting good grades at Edina Middle School. She is also on the varsity gymnastics team, and you should see that girl fly through the air, back flips and all, as she does her floor routine and the bars. She has many friends, and now, one boyfriend!

Joseph Mark, born January 18, 2003, is your next grandchild— I thought you might like that middle name. Rachel uses it quite a bit to keep him on the straight and narrow. But he is a good boy— affectionate, appreciative, and full of fun. He is also a top student in 2nd grade, reads adult books with ease, and is a genius at putting Lego projects together. He has the same nose as Sarah and has his dad's mouth and eyes. But he has your long, skinny, flat feet and brilliant mind. To my delight, Joe loves sports, watching and play-ing. I watched him play a basketball game for the first time recently and was amazed at his ball-handling ability. The best play was when he dribbled end to end and shot the ball from three-point land (if there was a three-point line) with an overhand baseball throw. There was nothing but net, as he helped preserve his team's victory. OK, so it was just a Saturday morning eight-year-old's game. But I was in heaven watching Joe.

Elizabeth Grace was born just ten days after Mike and Kelly moved to Sioux Falls from San Francisco, on July 14, 2003. What a delightful surprise, both to have them in town and to have a new grandchild. There is no getting around the fact that she is strong-willed and becomes upset easily if things aren't going quite right. But she is also sweet, smart, and very talented, speaking fluent Spanish, becoming a violin virtuoso, and taking piano, Chinese, golf, swim-ming, and tennis. No one can say she is not well-rounded. Her par-ents are eager to make sure all their children have ample opportunity to be well prepared for their place in the world.

On March 23, 2006, Luke was born. Unlike his sister, he is easy-going and happy most of the time, except when his feelings get hurt. He has a rather typical relationship with his sister, loving her and trying to do everything she does, but also engaging in a normal amount of daily disagreements. He is also a huge fan of Lego proj-ects, and the usual trucks, cars, planes, and all things inter-galactic. He is good-sized and active in soccer. I could see him involved in the other football game in the future. In the meantime, like his sister, he speaks fluent Spanish thanks to his morning nanny, Irma, from Columbia, and has begun a string instrument, the cello.

On December 24, 2008, I was sitting in church with Sarah J., when Elizabeth bounced into the pew, followed by her parents and brother. She was jumping up and down and bursting with im-portant information. Since she quite often jumps up and down and has something to share, I only half-listened to her news and nodded, uh-hmm.

"Mom," Sarah said, "Did you hear what she said?!"

"No," I said, and then said to Elizabeth, "What did you say?"

"Mom and Dad are going to have twins!!!"

I could scarcely believe my ears! Merry Christmas!!!

July 7, 2009, was the day our twins joined us in the world. Catherine came first and weighed about 5 pounds, 12 ounces. Christian followed immediately and weighed a few ounces more. They were perfect, and, of course, gorgeous beyond words. Kelly's mom and I brought Elizabeth and Luke to the hospital an hour later. Immediately they sat down near their mom and one baby was placed in each of their arms. "Oh," said Elizabeth, "I always knew about the babies, but I didn't know how much I would love them!"

Catherine is rather fearless, venturing to high places and resting comfortably in unknown arms. She has a sunny disposition and loves making funny expressions. She also loves to taste everything. Recently she developed a strong attachment to my golf cart and loves nothing more than riding through the neighborhoods. Like her sister, she knows what she wants, and screams in protest when the ride is over.

Christian loves trucks and running into things with his trucks. Sweet and affectionate, he loves to laugh and cannot get enough games of hide and seek. Looking at books and being read to is also a favorite occupation.

It still hurts my heart that you are not able to hug, cradle, and throw in the air these grandchildren. It is so unfair that you were deprived of this part of life, which you longed for way before any of your children were ready to give you grandchildren. But as you knew so well, life is not fair, and one can only go on, grateful for the life one has.

I hope you will see this book as a long open love letter to you and to your work, a love letter that will be read by those who knew you and admired your work and also by those who never knew you personally. A love letter that will infuse all who read it with the remarkable compassion you had for the world and the zest you brought to everything you did.

Beyond that, know that this book is my last love letter to you, to the life we shared and the love we nurtured. As our friend Tom Daschle quoted so appropriately:

> One brief moment, and all will be as it was before—
> Only better, infinitely happier, and forever—
> We will all be one together with Christ.

All my love,
Sandy

An Excerpt from
The Congressional Record
of the 105th Congress
from the United States Senate.
Presented by Senator Tom Daschle
on February 4, 1997

REV. MARK JERSTAD: A LIFE OF FAITH, GRACE AND
DIGNITY

Mr. Daschle. Mr. President, I want to take this opportunity
today to honor my dear friend, Rev. Mark Jerstad, a Lutheran pastor
and head of the Good Samaritan Society in Sioux Falls. After having
spent much of his adult life comforting the dying and grieving, Mark
recently learned that he has terminal colon cancer. This news was a
sad blow to all those who know and love him. Yet as we face the loss
of our friend, we are inspired by the strength of character shown by
Mark and his family.

Mark's ability to help others confront their fears and prepare
for their next journey has always been based on his strong faith in
God. Now it is this same faith that has enabled Mark to be at peace
with his own death. You see, Mark believes himself to be a lucky
man. Unlike many, he has the time to say goodbye, and to reflect
on the life he has led. As he says, we are nothing but the sum of our
deeds. I believe him, and by this measure Mark has lived a life of
kindness and love. We cannot help but grieve for the fact that Mark

will no longer be with us. We must grieve for his children, Rachel, Michael, and Sarah, who will be losing their father. And we must grieve for Sandy, who will lose her husband of 31 years. But we can be at peace knowing that Mark is living out his remaining days to the fullest. He is at peace, and with his loved ones.

Mark eloquently described the challenge we all face, "Unfortunately, people just can't seem to live life to the fullest until they come face to face with their own death and incorporate it into their own existence." Mark has done just that, continuing his work as the chief executive officer of the Good Samaritan Society of Sioux Falls while sharing his remaining precious days with friends and family from throughout the country. He is an example for us all.

Mark, we wish you and your family well. Let your faith, grace and dignity be a lesson to us all.

Mr. President, I ask the unanimous consent that the text of an article from the Sioux Falls Argus Leader, honoring Mark Jerstad be printed into the RECORD.

There being no objection, the article was ordered to be printed into the RECORD, as follows:

CEO Who Counseled the Dying Faces His Own Death with Faith
By Steve Young

Mark Jerstad sat in an X-Ray room at Sioux Valley Hospital in November when cold reality swept over him.

The chief executive officer of the Good Samaritan Society in Sioux Falls had just finished tests for what doctors thought might be an appendix problem.

He was waiting alone for the results to come back when he suddenly felt "like a peeled grape shaking in a snow bank at 40 degrees below zero."

The feeling lasted 30 seconds. When it passed this Lutheran pastor and business executive knew exactly what was wrong.

"All of a sudden, it came to me... almost like a voice," he recalls. "You have cancer, and it is terminal."

He was right.

Jerstad, 54, learned that he has an aggressive, advanced stage of colon cancer. There is no cure. There is only the hope that chemotherapy might prolong his life a month, maybe two.

But this isn't a story about one man dying. Rather, this is a tale about one man's incredible faith – and what it means to live in the shadow of your own mortality.

Lean and angular, Jerstad greets visitors in his spacious Good Samaritan office with the same firm handshake that has been his trademark.

Though the chemotherapy leaves him periodically weak, he still routinely comes to work to oversee affairs at the nonprofit monolith that provides services to senior citizens in 240 facilities in 26 states.

This has been Jerstad's job for 7 ½ years. He has been with Good Samaritan since 1985. Before that, he was campus pastor and a religion professor for nine years at Augustana College. And before that he served as a pastor in International Falls, Minn.

In many ways, those years of ministering to church members and college students helped prepare him for what lay ahead.

In International Falls, Jerstad counseled scores of people and their families through death and grief.

"Honestly, I think I was given a gift of working with dying people," he said. "I could be honest with them – someone who could be open-minded and listen and hear their fears."

So many times, he sat beside them at the moment of death, helping people in their journey from this existence to the next. It couldn't help but affect his own life.

"How can it not?" Jerstad says. "I mean, I believe we are the sum of our life's experiences. I really feel these very intimate sharings of people as they were dying have touched my life deeply and richly."

"They've helped me be at peace with my own dying, for sure."

Similarly, his years of teaching death and dying classes at Augustana helped prepare him as well.

Jerstad would share his experience in International Falls with his classes. But his focus was more on living than dying.

"When you think about it, we're all terminal... We're all dead men walking. We just don't know when that final day will be," he said.

"Unfortunately, people just can't seem to live life to the fullest until they come face to face with their own death and incorporate it into their own existence."

That isn't a problem for Jerstad. Indeed, there never has been a moment in the last three months when he bolted upright in bed in the middle of the night, sweating in fear about what awaits him.

Certain Sadness

Obviously, there is sadness. He looked forward to becoming a grandfather and baptizing his own grandchildren.

He thought maybe he would get to officiate at the marriages of his two daughters and his son—a possibility that now seems remote.

"You know, I kind of wish it was summer rather than winter," he said as he glanced out his office window. "I like to be able to sit out in my backyard in the afternoons and evenings, just watching the sun go down."

Still, Jerstad won't mire himself in what might have been. He is a man of the moment.

When he was diagnosed with cancer, he had to wait a couple

of days before undergoing colon surgery. So Jerstad got a discharge form, signed his name to it and checked himself out of Sioux Valley for the day.

He then drove out to Good Samaritan and attended the morning Bible study there. After sharing news about his cancer with co-workers and staff, he "went home to my kids, built a fire in the fireplace and just kind of hung out. It really was a wonderful time."

There have been many similar moments since. He talks about liking to begin each day by snuggling in bed with his wife, Sandy, and sharing a thought or two.

"Sometimes, I reach over and just touch her... and thank God for our partnership of 31 years."

He goes into the office most mornings and stays until the workday ends, or until he wears out.

Greeting old friends

In recent weeks, he has spent much time greeting old friends who have sought him out during his illness. One of them flew in recently from Alaska, another from Hawaii, yet a third came all the way from Johns Hopkins in Baltimore to spend 45 minutes with him.

"There was a tycoon I knew who wept like a child and embraced me," Jerstad said, his smile growing as he recounts the memory. "I was able to comfort him, and we both were able to grow through that experience."

That, he will tell you, is one of the joys about living when you are dying. It certainly makes him thankful that his life did not end suddenly, that he has had weeks and months to prepare.

Undoubtedly, Jerstad thinks a lot about what death will be like. But he doesn't fear it.

"One of the things that fires me up," he said, and his voice breaks as his eyes fill with tears, "is knowing I'll get a chance to meet my dad again. He died a couple of years ago. I loved him dearly."

What a glorious reunion, the son said. Yet until then, this husband and father intends to revel in the support of his family, his friends, and his faith – for as long as he has.

"I have to say, I wonder if I have been given a gift," Jerstad said, marveling at his own outlook. "I mean, I'm surely not in denial. If anyone has accepted the reality of their death much sooner than normal, it is I."

Gift of faith

How can it be? How can anyone face death with no resentment, anger or bitterness?

In a phrase he said with a smile, it is a gift.

"The gift of faith," Mark Jerstad said. "Maybe I'm not angry because I'm so hopeful for the life beyond this life.

"I'll be honest; I know my life is in the hands of the Lord. I can't fantasize anything better than that."

Time Line

1960   Mark graduates from Minnehaha Academy, Minneapolis, and begins his studies at St. Olaf College.

1962   Sandy graduates from Roosevelt High School, Virginia, Minnesota, and begins her studies at St. Olaf.

1963   Mark and Sandy meet casually and have their first date.

1964   Mark graduates from St. Olaf College with an English major, and begins studies at Luther Seminary.

1964   Mark and Sandy become engaged.

1965   Mark and Sandy are married in Virginia, Minnesota, on August 21, and move into a small basement apartment in St. Paul near Luther Seminary.

1966   Sandy graduates from St. Olaf College in three and a half years with an English education major and a Spanish minor.

1966-67 Mark interns at First Lutheran in West Seattle and Sandy teaches 9th grade English at an inner-city school.

1968   Mark graduates from Luther Seminary and applies for entry to Union Theological Seminary in Richmond, Virginia. He studies beginning and advanced Hebrew all summer. Sandy is pregnant.

1969   Rachel is born in Richmond, Virginia. Mark decides to take a call to a congregation instead of accepting the faculty invitation to join the doctoral program at Union. After six months at Sandy's mother's house in Virginia, Minnesota, Mark takes a call as assistant pastor at Zion Lutheran Church in International Falls, Minnesota.

1970   Mark becomes the only pastor after the departure of the senior pastor.

1971   Michael is born.

1972   Sarah is born.

1976   Mark takes a call to be Campus Pastor at Augustana College, in Sioux Falls, SD.

1977   Sandy is hired to coach the women's softball team at Augustana, while also teaching part-time at the state penitentiary.

Sandy is hired to coach the women's tennis team in the fall.

1979   Sandy is hired on full-time in the athletic department at Augustana College and begins work on a master's degree in health, education, and recreation.

1980   Sandy graduates from South Dakota State University with a master's degree.

1985   Mark goes to work at the Good Samaritan Society as head of Human Resources.

1987   Rachel graduates from high school and begins studies at Augustana.

1989   Mark is offered the job of President and CEO of the Good Samaritan Society and accepts.

Sandy begins studies at the University of South Dakota

while continuing all her coaching duties.

Mike graduates from high school and begins studies at Tufts University in Boston.

1991   Sandy's softball team wins a national championship.

Sarah graduates from high school and begins studies at St. Olaf College.

1993   Mike graduates from Tufts University.

Sandy's softball team wins second at nationals.

1994   Sandy graduates from the University of South Dakota with a doctorate in Educational Administration.

1995   Sarah graduates from St. Olaf College and is hired by the Bureau of Labor Statistics in Washington, DC.

Rachel graduates from Augsburg College, and goes to work at Northwestern Hospital.

1996

Mike graduates from Georgetown Law and begins work for Briggs and Morgan Law Firm, Minneapolis.

November 10. Mark is diagnosed with late stage colon cancer.

1997   March 29. Mark dies the night before Easter.

May. Sandy's softball team wins regionals and returns to nationals, tying for 7th place.

August 7. Sarah Kristin is born to Rachel.

1998   May. Kelly graduates from George Washington University Medical School.

June 6th. Mike and Kelly are married at Our Savior's Lutheran Church in Sioux Falls.

2003   January 18. Joseph Mark is born to Rachel.

Sandy retires from her coaching and teaching job at Augustana on July 1.

July 14. Elizabeth Grace is born to Mike and Kelly.

2004   Sarah receives her PhD in psychology from the University of Minnesota.

2006   March 23. Luke William is born to Mike and Kelly.

Sandy is elected to the South Dakota State Senate.

2009   July 7. Twins Catherine and Christian are born to Mike and Kelly.

2010   Sandy runs for the state senate a third time and is defeated.

2011   Sandy edits Mark's sermons and writes her reflections for this book.

Rachel's children: Sarah and Joe

Mike and Kelly's children: Elizabeth, Luke, Christian and Catherine

Sarah,   Mike,   Sandy,   Rachel   and Mark

Mark Jerstad, born in 1942 in Bagley, MN, graduated from St. Olaf College in 1964. Following graduation from Luther Seminary and Union Theological Seminary, he served as pastor at Zion Lutheran Church in International Falls, Minnesota. He was called to serve as campus pastor at Augustana College in Sious Falls, South Dakota, where he moved with his wife, Sandy, and three children, Rachel, Mike and Sarah in 1976. In 1985 he joined the Good Samaritan Society and in 1989 he was appointed President and CEO by the board of directors. In November, 1996, Mark was diagnosed with late stage colon cancer and died March 29, 1997.

Sandy Jerstad, born in 1943, graduated from St. Olaf College a year after marrying Mark in 1965. She taught junior high school geography and English before finding a career in athletics at Augustana College, coaching tennis and volleyball for six years and softball for 27 years. Her softball team won the NCAA Division II title in 1991. Sandy is in the Augustana Hall of Fame, The South Dakota Sports Hall of Fame, and the National Fastpitch Coach's Hall of Fame. She earned a doctorate in educational administration in 1994. Sandy served on the South Dakota State Senate for four years and continues to teach part-time at Augustana.

Printed in the USA
CPSIA information can be obtained
at www.ICGtesting.com
LVHW011124200324
775014LV00023B/255